# THE GREAT AMERICAN SERMON SURVEY

**DR. LORI CARRELL**

FOREWORD BY DR. DAVID R. MAINS

MAINSTAY
Church Resources
Helping Pastors Help People Grow

Acquisition Editor, Karen Mains.

Coordinating Editor, Brad Davis.

Produced by The Livingstone Corp. for Mainstay Church Resources. Project staff include Bruce Barton, Jonathan Farrar, Katie Gieser, Chris Hudson, and Linda Taylor.

Cover and interior design by Gary Gnidovic.

Mainstay Church Resources' passion is to facilitate revival among God's people by helping pastors help people develop healthy spiritual habits in nine vital areas that always characterize genuine times of spiritual awakening. To support this goal, Mainstay Church Resources pro-vides practical tools and resources, including the annual 50-Day Spiritual Adventure, the Sea-sonal Advent Celebration, and the Pastor's Toolkit.

Carrell, Lori.
Great American Sermon Survey/ Lori Carrell.
ISBN 1-57849-169-X
08 07 06 05 04 03 02 01 00 99
10 9 8 7 6 5 4 3 2 1
Printed in the United States of America

*This book is dedicated to
my children, Cheyenne and Cody,
and to all those who will listen to
sermons in the new millennium.*

*A special thanks to my editor, Karen Mains,
whose guidance was priceless.*

# Preface

## "What are you doing on your sabbatical?"

I have been asked this question over and over during the last year and a half. My first response is usually "taking a long nap," but if the inquirer demonstrates even a tiny bit of further interest, I launch into a passionate explanation of my sermon survey research. In my community of Oshkosh, Wisconsin, numerous local residents have endured my descriptions of this project. My dentist, chiropractor, beautician, and, yes, even my obstetrician. The other parents at T-ball, the custodian in the *Arts and Communication* building, our frequently visiting plumber, and numerous pizza deliverers, anxious to get on with their thirty-minute mandate. "Well," I think to myself, "they *did* ask."

Interestingly, of all those held temporarily hostage to my detailed description of this sermon survey research, only one has actually let her eyes glaze over as she retreated, saying, "I guess that might be interesting to someone who listens to preachers." (Oh yes, my dentist's response was simply, "Open wider, please.") So many of the others seemed to be waiting for me to take a breath—so they could launch into their own sermon stories: "Oh, you should have heard the sermon I heard last week . . ." Nearly everyone had a story to tell. Last week, I bumped into my obstetrician at T-ball, and he asked, "Is that book on sermons out yet? I want to read it and then pass it on to my preacher."

Listeners like to talk "sermon talk." Listeners are thrilled with a research premise that validates their perspectives and experiences as real and important. And when listeners were done telling their stories to me, they often asked me a follow-up question:

## "Why are you studying sermons?"

Raised on a steady diet of three sermons a week, I have been a listener myself for a very long time. Many of the sermons have been memorable, including a two-hour sermon delivered in the Yupiit Eskimo language in a small church on the Alaskan tundra, as well as the life-shaping inspiration of James Earl Massey in my college chapel.

As a Ph.D. in the discipline of Speech Communication, I have found it inevitable that my study of the spoken word would become intertwined with my thoughts about sermons. Over the years, as I have listened to other listeners dissect sermons and as I have conversed with preachers regarding their intentions, I could not help but notice a disparity in the perspectives of the listeners and the preachers. And, as a curious onlooker in a wide variety of types of churches, I began to hear two re-current themes from preachers: (1) "We are really teachers." (2) "Our sermons are counter-cultural." Since I teach and explore classroom communication and intercultural communication, my curiosity blossomed into research questions, which eventually became a sabbatical proposal.

The resulting project was supported by the University of Wisconsin-Oshkosh, which allowed a one-year sabbatical (1998–99) for my completion of this nation-wide, random-sample, "sermon survey" research titled, *The Communicative Act of Preaching*. The goal of this study was to compare and contrast preacher and listener perceptions of the communicative act commonly called the "sermon." **The communication perspective asserts that listeners and preachers are partners in interaction, mutually responsible for the co-creation of meaning during the sermon.**

Finding themselves engaged in discussion with an earnest researcher, some Oshkosh residents who dared to ask the "What?" and "Why?" questions about my sabbatical project, actually conversed with me long enough to become inquisitive about my methodology. (Of course, it may also have been that since I listened to their lengthy sermon stories, nodding with authentic interest, they felt a little obligated to continue the conversation.) At any rate, there were those who persisted long enough to ask,

## "How did you conduct the actual research?"

Then, of course, it became much more difficult to be brief. You see, in the year preceding the sabbatical, I engaged in an exploratory study, using an in-depth interview process with seventeen preachers and thirty of their listeners. Those preliminary preachers were selected for their diversity as well as their proximity to the research institution. From those interviews and extensive literature review, two survey instruments were generated: a fourteen-item preacher survey and a ten-item listener survey. A primary strength of this sermon survey research is that most *survey questions were open-ended*; listeners and preachers did not select from a list of limited answer options, but rather, were able to express their own thoughts in as much detail as they desired.

A total of 581 preachers and their listeners from churches across the United States participated in the sermon survey research. Importantly, the selection of preacher-participants was *random*. This random process selected participants whose combined responses yielded data that represented *typical* preachers in this country at the turn of the millennium.

To find the preachers and their listeners, I drew a random sample from a list updated by a para-church organization in 1997. Those randomly selected one thousand preachers were sent an explanation of the study (approved by the institutional review board at UW-Oshkosh), a survey, a postage-paid reply envelope, researcher contact information, and a sheet detailing levels of participation. Those levels of participation included: (1) do nothing; (2) complete the survey; (3) complete the survey and distribute listener surveys; (4) complete the survey and participate in an in-depth phone interview; or (5) complete the survey, distribute listener surveys, and participate in an in-depth phone interview. Participants were assured anonymity. Eighty-nine envelopes were returned as "undeliverable" or "no longer at this address." A total of 102 preachers completed surveys. Of those completing surveys, 88 involved their listeners as research participants and 64 provided in-depth interviews. A random survey of non-participant preachers found them citing either lack of time or wariness regarding research conducted by a secular institution as their primary reason for non-participation. Eighty-three percent of the preacher-participants were Protestant and 17 percent were Catholic; 84 percent were male and 16 percent were female.

The preacher-participants who distributed listener surveys were instructed to announce the participation opportunity publicly, and then to leave the listener surveys in an accessible area. Such methodology is necessary, as churches generally will not release their membership names and addresses to researchers. This listener selection process assured that all listener-participants were listening to a preacher-participant preach. There were 479 listeners who participated. An explanation of the study, survey, and postage-paid response envelope were stapled in a packet for each listener choosing to participate. Anonymity was assured as listeners returned their surveys directly to the researcher. Sixty percent of the listener-participants were Protestant and 40 percent were Catholic; 61 percent of the listeners were female and 39 percent were male. Unfortunately, a majority of listeners did not provide demographic information related to race/ethnicity, making this important variable unusable. Data were collected over a five-month period. Open-ended responses were analyzed and categories of responses were created. The categorical and inferential data were then analyzed quantitatively; the statistical results are reported throughout the book.

Preachers indicating willingness to be interviewed were contacted by phone to set an appointment time for the interview. The interviews were based on a further set of questions compiled in part based on the literature review and in part based on the survey responses. Interviews lasted a minimum of thirty minutes and were conducted over a period of four months. The interview results were analyzed qualitatively, resulting in the generation of response *themes*, which are reported in this book as well.

In the initial section of this book (*The Power of the Spoken Word*), I lay a foundation for approaching the sermon as a communicative act. In the second section (*Talk to One Another*), listener and preacher responses are presented, with a call for dialogue. *Time to Listen*, the third section, provides an opportunity for listeners and preachers to listen to those who study teacher communication as well as to improve their own ability to listen to each other. And finally, in section four (*Transformation*), I support the contention that for preachers and listeners to engage in sermon communication that is actually transformative, they will need to examine and perhaps transform their own communicative behavior.

Those few conversationalists who made it through my methodological mutterings often asked for the title of the book in which these results would be reported. "Well," I'd reply softly, ready to attribute the seemingly arrogant claim of the title to my ambitious editor, "It's tentatively titled, *The Great American Sermon Survey*."

"Great? What's so great about it?" probed just a few inquiring minds. What makes this sermon survey research potentially "great" is not its scope, budget, nor researcher, but rather its unusual theoretical perspective. Yes, a *communication* perspective, which asserts that the meanings made in the minds of the listeners are just as valid to study as the words of the preachers' sermons. If greatness exists, it flows from the transformative power of the spoken word used by humans to affect one another. Yes, indeed, the greatness can exist if listeners and their preachers begin to realize that sermon communication, like all communication, is a *mutual endeavor*.

# CONTENTS

# Introduction

to

*The Great American Sermon Survey*
Dr. David R. Mains

In 1967, along with a handful of idealistic friends, I planted a church in the inner city of Chicago. Disappointed with the state of the American church at that time, we began an experimental journey, a living laboratory which sought answers to the question: How can we make church vital in our contemporary culture?

Many who analyzed the attempts at Circle Church have said that our efforts were fifteen years (some said thirty years) ahead of our time. Though styles shift and approaches in church life are variable, the principles we discovered then have affected everything we have done in communications ministries during the years since we resigned from that pastorate in 1977.

One of my firmly held convictions, forged in the laboratory of that energetic time, was that preaching had to change if it was to communicate the gospel to our contemporary world.

Though called to preach, I began to realize I was a *communicator* of God's truths. I wondered, "How could the vital message of Scripture be connected in life-impacting ways to the minds and hearts of hearers?" This is the endless wrestling match for the church in all times, but it is particularly imperative for the church of the second millennium as we move from a word-oriented culture to a sight and sound generation. The media age is profoundly affecting the way we perceive and know truth.

This wrestling match began in the worship brainstorm sessions we held every week with staff and lay people at Circle Church. We were designing and re-designing worship services to make them meaningful, placing a high value on the discovery and use of the gifts of the lay people. In time I came to realize that the burden of

13

innovative and creative worship was not only lifted but improved when we freed our parishioners to plan and execute each week's service. An unanticipated benefit was remarkable improvement in the effect of my sermons.

Ten post cards went out each week inviting a rotating group of parishioners to brainstorm the worship service several Sundays ahead. By the evening of our meeting, I would have reduced the Scripture text to a key biblical truth. Around this single theme, we would design the service. In that dialogue with lay people, I the pastor often discovered that my thoughts were not where my people were living out their lives.

"That's a good idea, Pastor," someone might say, "but it doesn't really have any meaning to my daily struggles (I hope this doesn't offend you). Sometimes I think preachers basically preach to themselves. 'Atonement' is a great theological concept, but frankly, I need help dealing with lust. I think a lot of the guys in our church have the same problem, if they would just admit it."

So at my dining room table, I frequently abandoned the labor of a carefully constructed theme sentence and, with the help of my lay people, would rebuild a preaching message and a service that connected to the growth agonies they faced daily.

It turns out that it was not my seminary professors, but my lay people, who best taught me how to preach.

Not only did we engage in weekly sermon and worship brainstorm sessions, we (my preaching staff grew eventually into a team of communicators who shared the pulpit) offered an elective adult class after the morning service. Here anyone who had questions, challenges, or additional thoughts was invited to further discuss the meaning of the morning's theme. I remember asking one group what they thought I had been trying to say. A young student turned it around, "Actually, Pastor, I'm not sure. What do *you* think you were trying to say?" The truth was, I wasn't sure exactly what it was I wanted to say!

It was here that the concept of the theme sentence took hold— one succinct key biblical truth which included a life application and a way to bridge from the scriptural mandate to the everyday life of the listeners. Never again would I be caught not knowing exactly what it was I wanted to say.

These two tools—pre-service planning and dialogue with lay people and the essential feedback from those who have just listened to a sermon and attended worship—gave me a text to study alongside my holy Scriptures. This second text was the lives of my people. Ten years of talking with them, listening to them, and formulating preaching concepts alongside them turned me from a good preacher into a transformative communicator.

Dr. Lori Carrell, an award-winning professor of speech and cross-cultural communication, believes that the sermon is still a remarkable communication phenomenon in our sight and sound culture. She writes, "Yet even as technology explodes, there is one place where the face-to-face 'public speech' flourishes. . . .Where do people gather to hear someone they know speak publicly? In the United States, at the turn of the millenium, incredibly, that place is the church." And then she maintains, "The face-to-face spoken word is the most viable 'medium' for the communication of the Christian faith."

Dr. Carrell, while on sabbatical and funded partly by the University of Wisconsin in Oshkosh, conducted a sermon survey project which interviewed both pastors and lay people as to their perceptions about the role and effect of sermons in weekly life. What would your people say if a researcher asked them to tell her their opinions, beliefs, and attitudes about sermons? Would you have been as courageous as some of these Protestant pastors and Catholic priests who gave a secular university professor, a stranger to all, the go ahead to conduct this research work?

The results of *The Great American Sermon Survey* are remarkable! If your people—what they hear, how they hear, and what they want from weekly sermons—are important to you, then you need to read this book. Perhaps you will be persuaded to work to create what Dr. Carrell calls "co-creation of meaning" on Sunday mornings. Perhaps you will discover, as I did twenty years ago, that my lay people were one of my best resources in sermon preparation.

I guarantee you will come away convinced that the power of

words is potentially more transformative than we ever dreamed. I hope you will come away reminded that the sermon is indeed one of the most important activities you will do each week.

But this is not just a book for preachers. It is designed to help the preacher and the listener co-create meaning. Dr. Carrell gives a challenge to the lay person not to waste a lifetime of Sunday morning listening minutes. She draws on her academic discipline to teach listeners, hearers of the sermon, to become competent, active listeners, to realize that they bear mutual responsibility with the preacher to co-create shared communicative meaning. You may want to design classes for listening to sermons around the principles Dr. Carrell includes in chapters in this book.

It is important to remember that Dr. Carrell is not a seminary professor. She is a highly skilled communication expert who brings a refreshingly new slant to the understanding of how we speak and how we hear.

Today I am watching the emergence of concepts which bring new vitality to those who struggle to understand how to best communicate the gospel in our time. Much of this dialogue authenticates the principles I believed in so strongly when I was a young pastor building a church on the west side of Chicago in a teamster's union hall. My colleagues and lay people believed that the body of Christ could and should be more than what we saw around us at that time.

Dr. Lori Carrell's approach to the spoken word, and particularly sermons, is so much more articulate, professional (and delightful) than I could ever have imagined. She is a master of her discipline. How fortunate we are that she is passionate about the communicative process which occurs Sunday after Sunday in the churches of our land. She has many gifts to bring to those who prepare and also to those who listen to sermons.

My prayer is that we will be open to receive them.

# SECTION 1

# THE POWER OF THE SPOKEN WORD

*"Words are powerful; use them carefully."*
A LISTENER

Chapter 1

# We're in This Together

### The Preacher's Week

HAT A GREAT WEEK it had been. Pastor John had studied the text of his sermon all day Monday with only one interruption. No funerals, no weddings, no arguments with his teenager. (The kid was at camp.) No midnight phone calls resulting in re-arranged schedules. On Tuesday, he completed a rough draft. His afternoon ministry at the ecumenical food bank had included a conversation with an elderly man that became the perfect, relevant illustration for his third and final point. On Wednesday, during a break in the deacon's meeting, he'd been able to discuss the text with an insightful friend who offered a valuable suggestion John inserted as an "application" section. Thursday, he spent time in prayer, and enjoyed a phone call with a colleague who was (coincidentally) preaching on the same text in a neighboring state. More revisions. Friday morning, he rehearsed in the pulpit, and spent time praying from the pews for each listener, asking for the Holy Spirit's guidance. A surprisingly good night's sleep on Saturday, morning devotional meditation on Sunday, and he was ready to preach.

### A Listener's Week

It had been a terrible week for Susan. Juggling the responsibilities of elderly parent care and child care, she'd missed an important deadline at work and hadn't had a conversation of more than three-minutes duration with her husband since Tuesday. Saturday night, after yelling at her children and apologizing over and over, she was convinced by a midnight panic attack that something had to change, but she didn't know what or how. Life circumstances seemed more powerful than her faith. The practical realities of her overwhelmed existence seemed far from the peace, joy, love, patience, gentleness, goodness, and self-control she knew should be a result of her spiritual journey. Next morning, she took the kids to their classes, then slipped into a pew. The music was soothing. The warm glow of smiles from loving friends encompassed her as she glanced around the congregation. And Pastor John's preaching—uplifting, relevant, practical, positive, and scriptural. What a moment, a message she would never forget. New-found hope. Fresh insight. Reassurance and challenge. As she walked to her children's classroom, she knew this week would be different— she would be different.

## Do Sermons Still Communicate?

Two lovely scenarios, but I can almost hear the voices of objection. "Wait a minute. Hang on." Preachers and listeners may be thinking, "Well, it's possible. But, it just doesn't *usually* work that way. Preachers don't have that kind of prep time; listeners' lives and sermon topics can't always be connected; dramatic transformations of listeners or communities are rare." Wait a minute. Let's get real.

In Christian churches across the United States, hundreds of thousands of preachers and millions of listeners participate in the communicative act of preaching. The face-to-face mode of public speaking (which dominated the political scene for much of this country's history) is now an unusual kind of presentation. How many people have heard a candidate speak "in person" before casting a vote for or against? Very few. Beginning with the Nixon–Kennedy presidential debates and continuing at this moment, most public speaking by leaders is now mediated by technology. With digital television and the Internet, "public communication" will need re-definition in Webster's next edition. We can take a college course via the Internet, "chat" globally with "rooms" full of people, and build virtual communities—all without one face-to-face encounter. To many, such possibilities are exciting as we enter the new millennium; to others, such change brings fear as we wonder if something of our humanity will be lost in this period of rapidly expanding technologies.

Marshall McLuhan's contention that the electronic age would create a global village and would, at its very least, change our ways of thinking and knowing sounded prophetic. "Electronic technology," he claimed in the opening words of *The Medium is the Message*, ". . . is forcing us to reconsider and re-evaluate practically every thought, every action, and every institution."[1] In the church context, reconsideration of public speaking is consequentially legitimate. In this electronic age, as faceless relationships via chat rooms have become reality, we are forced to recognize that things have changed.

Whether they've read McLuhan's work or not, some technology users, on the edge of their seats anticipating the next hardware development, seem to also be insisting that face-to-face *public* communication will become an outdated mode of interaction. There are those in academia, certainly, who are planning the advent of virtual universities with a simple and precise justification: access to education for more people, benefit to the intellectual lives of masses. Yes, the new media are powerful; the magnitude of "audience size" increasing exponentially is mind-boggling. In the educational context, questions of quantity of learners versus quality of learning are being asked in the research. Grant monies are readily available for the formulation of programs that place technology between teachers and students.

Yet even as technology use explodes, there is one place where the face-to-face public speech flourishes. Not as the special event of a motivational speaker, passionately communicating her formula for success and then boarding the plane for the next town on the trail. Not as the modern-day Professor Hill, bringing his band instruments, or anti-aging cream, or "no-hungries" diet plan, to peddle with splendid speeches to a community group. Where do people gather to hear someone they know speak publicly? Where do they go to try to satisfy their craving for the early rhetorician's ideal—a good person speaking well about something that matters? Where is it they come, hoping to hear a credible speaker provide inspiration, information, and insight? In the United States, at the turn of the millennium, incredibly, that place is the church.

**The face-to-face spoken word is the most viable "medium" for the communication of the Christian faith.** This claim, made by renowned thinker Walter Ong, was part of his broader contention that different media accomplish different purposes.[2] In a recent reflection on Ong's ideas, homiletics professor David Buttrick echoes Ong while remaining mindful of McLuhan, "Speech may well be the singularly appropriate human medium for the proclamation of the gospel . . . So we will preach, but of course, we will preach *differently* in an electronic age."[3]

Suggesting that perhaps "rationality" is diminished in the electronic age because we "lose linear thinking," Buttrick warns that the electronic age has created listeners who have begun to value such decidedly non-linear thinking as multiple perspective taking, language which evokes visual images, and the power of story. While television uses visual images, multiple camera angles, and the drama of human experiences, television did not create our related mental capacities. Such capacities are provided through language. Such capacities are not new. "Rationality" is not threatened by our use of non-linear thought. For example, a sequential, deductive, topical main point sermon is not the only way to be rational, to use spoken language to communicate the gospel with other human beings. Preferred by some preachers trained in such a tradition? Sure, but deductive organizational patterns with topical main points are not more "spiritual" than other organizational patterns, nor are they modeled by Jesus or otherwise "recommended" in the Bible. There are many paths to rationality. Buttrick concludes his essay by recommending, "We are called to a profound act of reconceptualization. We are changing . . . Electronic media are impacting our lives. Perhaps, now we can at least begin with awareness."[4] McLuhan would probably have been pleased; after all, he was the one who announced, "I am absolutely opposed to all innovation, all change, but I am determined to understand what's happening."[5] Determining to *understand what's happening* seems appropriate for preachers and listeners as well.

Perhaps technology can serve an amazingly helpful function—provoking our awareness of the dynamism of words spoken and words thought. Perhaps technology can remind us of the related human appreciation of all that symbolic language makes possible: poetry and metaphor (the Psalms), multiple perspectives (the Gospels), culturally relevant narratives (Jesus' parables), epic drama (the Exodus) and "mediated interaction" (Jacob's dream and Mary's angelic visit).

As we seek understanding in the electronic age, why should we conclude that media use us, becoming more powerful than the human mind that created them? Such a world would make for an intriguing novel or film, but such a world is not inevitable. What about a slow, barely noticeable erosion of the value of the spoken word? It's possible, certainly. Listeners could demand shorter and shorter sermons; preachers could defer to new technologies, replacing the shortened "preach" with a five-minute clip of a prerecorded sound and light extravaganza or an interactive e-mail visit with Christians around the globe. Actually, such creativity might be refreshing on occasion, but it is neither fair nor accurate to suggest (as did McLuhan) that U.S. citizens are in the process of *outgrowing* the power of a face-to-face public speech because we've developed alternative technological devices.

Diminishing the power of the spoken word with new technologies is only imminent if we choose such a route, if we allow the disintegration of face-to-face public interaction. Might we? Yes. Must we? No. Should we? Will we? These are questions worthy of our thoughts and actions as we examine the vitality of preaching at the turn of the millennium. For now, the reality is that face-to-face public communication between preachers and listeners continues to involve millions of participants.

While there are those who preach via technology, when television and preachers are merged the popular response seems to be one of distrust. The term "tele-evangelist" has become the punch line for a good many jokes. This theme of distrust may have developed based on the unethical behavior of a few power-intoxicated tele-evangelists, but it is primarily promulgated via the medium itself. Electronic media serve as a distancing device between preacher and listener. Because television allows us to "receive" spoken words devoid of a relationship with the speaker, our ability to discern speaker credibility is diminished. With Internet interaction, we lose nonverbal cues to sincerity altogether. While a few widely known, credible preachers (such as Billy Graham) may be allowed the mechanism of television by their listeners, the phenomenon of preaching requires credibility that comes from listener and speaker being part of a "community"—the community of the church.

We are savvy consumers of media, able to desensitize ourselves to depicted fictional violence while still maintaining deep horror for real violence. Our experiences with media have taught us to withhold trust—we disbelieve commercials, though we apparently may still be affected by them. We are quick to question those who deliver a sermon through the medium of the airwaves. While such distrust is not always deserved, it is a real perception of many viewers. Trust is enhanced by relationship; relationship is diminished when interaction is not face-to-face. Fortunately, at this point in history, most sermons are still delivered face-to-face.

To discern whether or not a speaker has self-serving motives is actually an important component of critical thinking. Credibility of speaker and effective persuasion are highly related. The authors of *Persuasion and Influence in American Life,* Gary Woodward and Robert Denton Jr., tell us, "The power to persuade is often contingent on assessments of the credibility or authority of a source."[6] Our need to trust a speaker has been present since Aristotle approached the lectern. Aristotle's lectures focused on "persuasive rhetoric." In 335 B.C., he proposed three components of persuasion: *ethos* (personal character of the speaker), *pathos* (the ability to arouse emotions), and *logos* (the logic of the argument). Says current day communication scholar Sarah Trenholm, "In discussing *ethos*, Aristotle became one of the first communication specialists to point out the importance of source credibility."[7] Of course, he was not the last, nor have the developing media changed the basic nature of persuasion.

## The Sermon Is a Unique Public Speaking Event

The face-to-face sermon speech is a unique communication event. Why?

(1) Preachers live with demanding credibility expectations.

(2) Preachers are challenged—in their role as "messengers of God"—to preach messages to people with whom they are in relationship.

(3) Preachers are expected to tie each sermon topic to Scripture.

### Credibility

As listeners, we are in relationship with the speaker. While the relationship between preacher and listener is often that of "acquaintance" rather than "close or intimate friend," it is, nevertheless, a relationship. The preacher is the leader of a community; many of the preachers interviewed for this sermon survey research called themselves "servant leaders" and some used the word "facilitator." Regardless of the type of leadership, the preacher's life is observable. In no other public speech is the *demand for credibility* so high.

Who among us has not heard the phrase, "Practice what you preach"? If the preacher is parent to a teenager who is arrested for possession of crack cocaine (or is otherwise visibly defiant of authority), some church communities will use Scripture to say the preacher should resign. The demand for credibility is high; the pressure from such a standard is intense. One preacher tells of a divided church that resulted from a deck of playing cards noticed in his home. A listener recounts, "He told us in a sermon that we should not eat out on Sundays. Then he left church and went straight to Dairy Queen." Another pastor says, "My kids really feel the scrutiny at school. People expect a higher standard from the preacher and the preacher's family than they do from themselves." We don't really know if the dynamic weight loss speaker goes on to the next engagement with pizza breath and a hoard of Hershey's kisses hidden in a hubcap, but we are at least somewhat aware of our preacher's behavior. Listeners watch the preacher's life. Listeners talk to each other if potential hypocrisy is detected. Said one staff member–listener, "Everything he says in his sermons about building community, loving and respecting others, sounds good. But I see him weekly in staff meetings. I *know* how he treats others." Certainly the impact of preachers who are involved in financial fraud, emotional manipulation, or sexual abuse can scar a group of listeners for decades. One minister replacing another who had "fallen" said, "It took about eighteen months before anyone would even look me in the face, let alone trust me."

### God's Messenger

In part, this demand for observable credibility from the speaker is present because preachers both have been assigned and have taken on the role of *Messenger of God*. While church doctrines vary in their explanation of this phrase, it is an integral part of the tradition of preaching for the preacher to be characterized as speaking God's words, proclaiming messages from God to the people. Says one preacher, "My denomination wants us to really push homosexuality as a created, appropriate, alternative lifestyle. I'm not going to touch that in the pulpit. I believe and preach God's love for all, but I'm actually undecided about how to approach this complex issue. A statement from me, from the pulpit, will be taken as 'God's word.' " The responsibility of accepting such a speaking role must be sobering. Said another preacher, "It amazes me that someone could preach without prayer. How else can preachers be sure their messages are from God? Don't they understand the accountability we have to our congregations?" Seventeen percent of the listeners in this sermon research study suggested that preachers "work on their own spiritual lives, pray more, be God-centered, not self-centered, and ask themselves 'What would Jesus do?' " Listeners want to be sure their preachers are indeed bringing a message of God. Another said, "We put a lot of stock into what you say. Be sure it is God-directed."

### Use of Scripture

Finally, the sermon is unique from other public speaking in the expectation that preachers will *use specific portions of the Bible or themes from the Bible as primary source material every time.* Education for preachers involves rigorous study of the Scriptures, yet many listeners provide the following kind of statement when asked to give one message to all preachers in the United States: "Be Biblical. I often have trouble figuring out how the message and the Scripture passage are connected." One of the most commonly identified characteristics of a good sermon, according to surveyed listeners, was that it be "Scripture based"; a primary characteristic of a bad sermon was an unclear relationship between the Scripture passage and the key point(s) of the sermon.

While many denominations allow preachers freedom to choose Biblical texts, many others provide a lectionary of texts for preachers to use each week of the year. Preachers from these two types of traditions support their approach with the same argument. The preacher with a lectionary says, "I am sure to preach the 'whole counsel' of God. Otherwise I might neglect portions of the Bible which I find confusing, controversial, or just plain irrelevant." The preacher without a lectionary says, "I can preach systematically through books of the Bible—not an assigned verse here and a passage there. That way, I can be sure I don't favor my own agenda. I can be sure I am preaching the 'whole counsel' of God."

One preacher said she disciplined herself by "preaching from the Old Testament for the first three years of my ministry, and from the New Testament for the second three years." Another preacher admitted to spending eighteen months preaching through the Gospel of John. A listener complained of enduring a two-year series on Revelation. With or without a lectionary, many preachers sigh as they say, "Topic selection is a challenge."

Beyond the lectionary and the exegetical preacher (explaining verse by verse, passage by passage, or book by book) are the "topical" preachers who select a topic they think is important or needed, supporting that topic with passages or themes they choose from the Bible. This "needs-based" or "where the Spirit leads" topic selection process seems to receive the most criticism from other preachers because of the potential for preachers to neglect some topics and favor others. Yet listeners complain that even with a lectionary, "My preacher can work his pet topic into nearly any passage of Scripture." Said many listeners when advising preachers, "Don't push your own agenda."

The goal of *The Great American Sermon Survey* is to enable preachers and listeners who participate in this unique public communication event we call "preaching" to better understand each other. Randomly selected preachers and their listeners from across the country share their ideas and thoughts about preaching. It should be emphasized that the preachers were *randomly selected*; they are "typical" preachers, the kinds most of us listeners encounter when we go to church. Talking with preachers and listeners was fascinating. The tele-evangelist image of preachers as power-hungry, insincere manipulators was blown to bits. In conversation, preachers demonstrated their humor, their sincerity, their concern for their listeners. While they talked freely about frustrations, most were optimists, committed to making a difference. Many were cautious about change. Regardless of their place on the conservative to liberal continuum, almost all interviewed preachers perceive themselves—and their messages—as counter-culture.

What about listeners? Bored automatons, trudging to church out of duty? Attention spans and intellects dulled by television viewing? Enduring condemnation week after week? No way. Those stereotypes don't hold up either. When asked if she could recall something she gained from a specific sermon, one listener from the Midwest said, "I love sermons. I could tell you a thousand things!" Said another, "Every sermon Father gives touches what is most human in us and lifts us up to what is heavenly." And a senior citizen said she listens to sermons because "I like to feel stimulated by new thinking. I hope to gain new insight into universal problems." Several listeners are able to point to specific times in their lives—a disappointment, a divorce, an overwhelming circumstance—during which words from a preacher saved them from desperation, despondency, and even death. Still others were led from unbelief to belief through a preacher's words from the pulpit and consider that decision to have been life changing. A few listeners even describe how a practical suggestion they heard in a sermon catapulted their church, and eventually their whole community, into action.

Of course, not all listeners have consistently had such positive experiences. And some preachers are overwhelmed by their daunting task, minimal responses, and unrealistic role expectations. Yet preachers keep preaching and listeners keep listening. An outsider looking in might rightly ask, "Why do you listen? Why do you preach? What are you expecting?" To be sure, some are not expecting much. Said one listener, "I listen to the sermon because it's part of the service. I gave up hoping for much a long time ago." A preacher from the Midwest freely admits, "My listeners come for worship, for friends, for music—not to hear a sermon." It is this kind of cycle of low expectation, which preachers and listeners can perpetuate, that is most dangerous to the survival of face-to-face public speaking in the church context.

In an introduction to their recent book, preachers Roger Alling and David Schlafer even assert as "common knowledge" that "the brute experiential fact remains, however, both for those who try to sit through sermons, and for those who try to deliver them: Many sermons just don't work."[8] One wearied listener concludes, "After 56 years of steady church-going there is *nothing* in my spirituality that I can attribute to a sermon. Everything good came from one-on-one contact outside the church service." A preacher's comment corresponds, "When I first became a pastor, I took the preaching thing very seriously. Now, I don't. . . . [More can happen] through private conversation." In fact, 57 percent of preachers participating in this sermon research say that preaching is *not* the most important part of their job duties. Indeed, 32 percent of listeners could not recall anything they "gained from a specific sermon."

In his book, *Preaching with Spiritual Passion: How to Stay Fresh in Your Calling*, pastor Ed Rowell admits that among preachers, sometimes "there's a deeper cynicism, the suspicion at our soul's core that the sermon we prepared and delivered with such hopeful anticipation went largely unheard. Maybe the big joke of the universe is they've all gone largely unheard."[9] Others echo such sentiments. Michael B. Regele, author of *Death of the Church*, states in an interview, "Many churches are content . . . It is time to stop this denial and confess that our strategies have not worked. Church leaders are working harder and harder for fewer positive results."[10] Those outside the church context, particularly academics, claim often and loudly that church processes like the sermon do not motivate listeners to change themselves or to become change agents in their cultural systems. For example, in his book, *The Comfortable Pew*, Pierre Burton accuses preachers and church-going listeners of "reinforcing the status quo" of the unjust cultural system, rather than challenging it. In essence, he asserts that the impact of sermons is limited to affirmation that everything is just fine the way it is.[11] The Barna Research Group recently reported a study which found no difference between Christians and non-Christians in either moral behavior choices or provision of assistance to the poor and hungry.[12]

So does the communicative act of preaching make a difference? Now more preachers and listeners are squirming in their reading chairs. "Hang on," they say, "Preaching can make a difference! Think of all those great preachers who changed the history and direction of various segments of the church. Think of those amazing preachers mobilizing listeners against injustice. Remember my preacher, the one who loved me into faith in Jesus, who deepened my spiritual journey." One pastor remarked, "Preaching is really a vital part of my pastoral care." Thirty-five percent of listeners in this study say the sermon "impacts my spiritual life" more than any other part of the church experience. Ed Rowell, discarding his previous (and admittedly occasional) cynicism, proclaims strong and loud, "Preaching matters, preaching changes lives, preaching is a big deal."[13] How does preaching matter? In what way are lives changing? And indeed, what is the big deal? Those are the questions of this study. This book reports the answers, from both listener and preacher perspectives.

Why both perspectives? Because **preaching is a communicative act.** For that reason, *The Great American Sermon Survey* involves "looking through the lens" of *communication*. This study was not conducted by a theologian, a homiletics professor, or a preacher, but rather by a researcher of human communication. The study of preaching is not new, but the study of preaching as "communication" is not typical. Homiletics books are written by preachers for preachers about preaching. Such "inside" perspectives are absolutely unrivaled in value. This research offers another perspective, equally unrivaled in value. So now, as we begin our examination of the sermon through a distinctively different lens, let's ask, "How is a communication perspective distinct?"

## Notes

[1] McLuhan, M. & Fiore, Q. (1967). *The medium is the message.* New York: Random House, 8.

[2] Ong, W. (1967). *The presence of the word: Some prolegomena for cultural and religious history.* New Haven: Yale University Press.

[3] Buttrick, D. (1993). "Preaching to the faith in America." In L.I. Sweet (Ed.), *Communication and change in American religious history* (pp. 302–319). Grand Rapids, MI: Wm. B. Eerdmans Publishing Co.

[4] See Buttrick, 319.

[5] McLuhan, M. (1996). *This hour has seven days.* CBS Television.

[6] Woodward, G.C., & Denton, R.E. Jr. (1996). *Persuasion and influence in American life* (3rd ed.). Prospect Heights, IL: Waveland Press, 116.

[7] Trenholm, S. (1995). *Thinking through communication: An introduction to the study of human communication.* Boston: Allyn & Bacon, 5.

[8] Alling, R., & Schlafer, D.J. (Eds.). (1997). *Preaching as the art of sacred conversation: Sermons that work VI.* Harrisburg, PA: Morehouse Publishing, xi.

[9] Rowell, E. (1998). *Preaching with spiritual passion: How to stay fresh in your calling.* Minneapolis, MN: Bethany House Publishers, 35.

[10] Allender, D., Huttchum, K., & Hancock, S. (1998). "Death of the church: A conversation with Michael B. Regele," *Mars Hill Review*, 11, 65–67.

[11] Burton, P. (1967). *The comfortable pew.* New York: J.P Lippincott Company, 80–81.

[12] Barna, G. (1999, January). Report to the Promise Keepers Organization, Colorado Springs, CO. Same study was also documented in October 27, 1998 news release with contact person David Kinnaman listed, phone number (805) 658-8885.

[13] See Rowell, 10.

Chapter 2

# The Co-creation
# of Meaning

O
NE SUNDAY DURING the sermon,
a child settled in with her crayons
and children's bulletin. Seated next
to her mother, this four-year-old
glanced around at the adults in the pews, played
a game of peek-a-boo with the "grandpa" behind
her, and inspected her elbows. Finally, she noticed the preacher way down in front. "Momma,"
she whispered, "Who is that man talking to?"
Yes, who indeed? The child could not detect the connection between the preacher, the spoken words of the sermon, and those
seated around her.

As a professor of speech communication, I have the privilege of
spending my professional life in continual exploration of that process which connects humans to one another. My teaching and research have an unchanging focus: the power of the spoken word.
Whether I'm working to enable teachers to improve their abilities
to connect with students whose cultures differ from their own,
assisting a novice public speaker with the organizational structure
of a persuasive speech to a hostile audience, or modeling mediation skills for students in a conflict management course, my work
is founded on a central premise: **Human communication is the
process of individuals together co-creating meaning; the process
of *connection*.**

There are literally dozens of definitions of communication

emanating from various kinds of thinkers—psychologists, technicians, sociologists, and communication scholars. In the seventies, communication scholar Frank Dance had catalogued 126 published definitions of the term.[1] Of course, more have been developed since that time. Each definition provokes our thinking in slightly different directions. Here is a sampling:

(1) Communication is a *process* whereby people *assign meanings* to stimuli in order to make sense of the world.[2]

(2) *Speech* communication is a human *process* through which we make sense out of the world and share that sense with others.[3]

(3) Spoken symbolic interaction is the *process* by which people use words and other *symbols* to create meaning and to *affect* one another.[4]

While all three definitions (representing three major schools of thought) agree that human communication is a "process" rather than an action with a reaction, each definition offers something unique. The first definition suggests that human communication can be unintentional; if you yawn during a sermon, trying to conceal the yawn, the preacher may notice and perceive that you are bored. You did not intentionally "send a message," but your behavior was given meaning. While some definitions of communication exclude *unintentional* communicating, so much of what we communicate is not planned. For example: "How could he think *that* comment was 'hate speech'?" or "Yes, I do care. I'm just really tired so my voice sounds like I don't."

"Incredibly valuable!" Those are the words we might choose for a headline to describe a study of communication that helps us become aware of the meanings people are attributing to our spoken words and accompanying nonverbal behaviors. While we must acknowledge that we cannot control all perceptions, we do well to develop self-awareness. For example, dozens of listeners in this sermon survey research ask preachers to quit using preacher jargon—"seminary talk." Many of those listeners make the assumption that preachers select such words to demonstrate their spiritual superiority; yet, many preachers are not even aware that they are using jargon. They speak the words they think with—selecting words based on clarity and precision. To learn to consider the perceptions of their listeners and then to alter word choice with the goal of *listener* clarity could be a profoundly meaningful change. Of course, discerning which words are considered "jargon" (without becoming condescending) would require a process of preachers listening to listeners, a process based on the acceptance that the perceptions of listeners are real, not wrong or right.

The second definition ("*Speech* communication is a human *process* through which we make sense out of the world and share that sense with others"[5]) shifts our focus to our uniquely human capacity that includes the fusion of *speech* (a genetic ability to shape air into specific sounds) and *language* (the culturally derived meanings attached to the sounds of speech).[6] Animals that talk are common in fairy tales and Disney movies. With talk, animals "become" human, able to predict the consequences of their actions, able to plan revenge, to forgive, and even to create award-winning song and dance. Of course, Simba and his buddies (in Disney's *The Lion King*) would not be nearly so intriguing if limited to growling. Spoken language is uniquely human.

Certainly, such reasoning does not extend to the offensive suggestion that those who are mute are "less human"—for in the absence of speech, other symbol systems develop. Our brains are hard-wired for symbol-use.[7] It is the specificity of this second definition that sets well with those of us who study the spoken word; we claim this discipline as the study of a uniquely human behavior. This second definition may remind preachers and their listeners of the potential power of the spoken word, grounded in our distinctive ability to use symbols to create meaning with others.

The third definition ("Spoken symbolic interaction is the *process* by which people use words and other *symbols* to create meaning and to *affect* one another"[8]) gets at the heart of speech communication, its function, which is to "affect one another." In his book, *How Real is Real*, Paul Watzlawick contends that our perceptions of reality are not just shaped, but are *created*, by the words we use to make meaning with others.[9] When a friend describes a beautiful sunset, a picture and a feeling are created in your mind. His words enable you to make meaning. When a parent reacts to a child's artwork, meaning is created between child and parent, meaning which can affect the child's self-concept for a lifetime. When a lie is spoken, a false reality is constructed that, once discovered, can rupture relationships. For example, when Bill Clinton's inner circle believed his lie, their minds accepted an "unreal reality." Their eventual discovery of the truth, and resulting feelings of betrayal, were probably more dramatic than those who never believed Clinton in the first place. This power to affect one another is serious business. Our spoken words shape the reality of those with whom we interact.

The words of a sermon, or the signed interpretation of those words, allow human beings to make meanings. As we make meanings, we allow ourselves to be affected. This basic function of human communication lies at the heart of communication, and so it also lies at the very heart of preaching. Without this function, human communication would lose its strength.

Hopefully, considering these differing definitions is broadening your thinking about human communication. Grounding ourselves in a communication perspective brings new insight to our understanding of preaching. Basic agreement about the meaning of the word "communication" is necessary before we proceed.

In a recent interview for *Preaching* magazine, a pastor of a large church was asked, "Who are the most effective communicators of the gospel to this culture?" The preacher (perhaps in defense of his often criticized seeker-sensitive approach) responded, "I . . . [am] . . . drawing up a very short list because it is one thing to be a good preacher. It is a second thing to be a good communicator. Preaching and communicating are two different things."[10] From a communication perspective, I must say that such a differentiation between the processes of preaching and communicating is fundamentally flawed. **All preachers and listeners are engaged in communication as they co-create meaning during the sermon.**

In addition, the implication that preachers who are doing well would necessarily be "known" nationally feels to me a little like fingernails on a chalkboard; many excellent preachers don't even seek large congregations, let alone notoriety. One preacher in this study was not on the identified "short list," but he has been combating racism and poverty, inspiring young people to careers that make a difference, as well as loving and serving listener-friends in tiny communities in the Southwest for more than sixty years. From one little church in a mining camp, dozens of his young listeners came to faith and are now leaders in politics, academia, social work, education, and other churches. Rather than a short list of recognizable names, listeners from across the nation could certainly draw up a long list naming communicating preachers whose effect was deep, spiritual, and lasting. If the spoken words of a sermon have an effect on a listener, that preacher is communicating.

The preacher quoted in the magazine as saying that "preaching and communicating are two different things" clarifies his remark by saying that his short list of communicators is comprised of preachers who can "actually engage the culture." He suggests that preachers who preach to church-going believers are not communicators, implying that "engaging the culture" is not necessary in sermons to believers. From a communication perspective, engaging the culture of their listeners is mandatory, a responsibility of all preachers.

What is culture? Culture is the set of meanings we create and share with others in our environment. For instance, how do you know how far apart to stand from a stranger—and how the rules change in an elevator? Your culture has taught you. Do you value work or leisure more? Do you plan to care for your elderly parents in your own home until their death? How do you define success? Your cultural system has shaped your answers to those questions.

*Life* magazine reports that 96 percent of U.S. citizens believe in God.[11] Yes, many will question the type, quality, and depth of that 96 percent's belief, but preaching to unbelievers is a less common phenomenon than preaching to believers. And believing listeners are not hermits, living without culture, unaffected by culture. Connecting to culture is *necessary* for ministering to believers, motivating believers, and mobilizing believers in a way that leads to individual, church, and cultural transformation. These are the tasks of preaching. And such tasks cannot be accomplished without communication that comes through the preaching of God's Word.

Before offering several insightful suggestions, authors of a recent sermon book lament that the church is "culture's victim [because] . . . the sermon as a monologue may be experiencing its last days. . . . [Current and future] generations . . . will no longer find it meaningful to be talked at for fifteen minutes. Congregations will expect to be engaged as a partner in the sermonic experience."[12] Expect to be engaged as a partner? You better believe it! The very definition of human communication as the "*co*-creation of meaning" asserts that the process is a *mutual* endeavor. Despite our misconceptions, the sermon has never been and will never be a monologue; yet it has been perceived as monologue, studied as monologue, and taught as monologue. If only the many collections of "great sermons" had also included listeners' descriptions of the effect of each sermon on their lives, churches, communities, or cultures, we would understand just how incorrect the monologue approach really is. We must not forget the function of human communication: We affect one another.

Though they might not use the M-word, there are preachers who approach their sermons as monologue. Said one preacher, "I guess I don't really know the needs of people in my church. I really don't know them at all." And another, when asked how he could detect the responsiveness of his listeners during the sermon said, "I guess I never really notice them. I'm concentrating on my sermon." Perhaps the traditions of their church culture have taught some preachers that they alone are to create meaning and distribute it. Perhaps the silence of their listeners has reinforced the monologic approach.

Even listeners may attend expecting a monologue. Of the 78 percent of surveyed listeners who don't talk to their preacher about the sermon, 24 percent say that such a process is not appropriate since the sermon is the "job" of the preacher. Said one listener, "I can't make sense out of the sermon usually, but I just don't know much about religion like the preacher does." Many listeners remarked, "Who am I to question a preacher?" Even if listeners provide verbal feedback, giving that "good sermon" comment at the door with a handshake or motivating the minister with "Amen!" and "Preach it, now, preach it!" comments, the meanings we've made, the places our minds have been during that sermon, are not made known. Let's try a triple negative: *Not* providing discernible or verbal response does *not* mean we listeners have *not* made meaning from the sermon! We have. Perhaps we've decided there is no relevance to our religion or that priests just don't understand our lives. Perhaps we've decided that we're giving away all our possessions right after church. Even as we quietly make meanings in our minds, we defy the monologue stereotype. We listeners are not mere spectators. Several listeners said the one message they would like to get across to all preachers is: "Preach with us, not at us."

It's not just the listeners; many preachers are dissatisfied with a "one-way" perception of preaching as well. Admitted one Southern pastor, "Preachers can be the loneliest people in the world." Still another preacher claimed, "Most preachers would preach themselves to death if someone just encouraged them a little." One preacher resonated with the communication perspective of *The Great American Sermon Survey:* "A good sermon is two-way communication. Just because you are sitting still and I am moving around doesn't mean it's all up to me. The message is a compilation of our lives together." A listener from across the country almost "Amened," saying, "In a good sermon, the preacher is talking with an audience, including them in the message so they have the opportunity to mentally participate." Authors of a recent book for preachers declare, "Good preaching does not simply issue reports about God's sacred conversations. Rather, good preaching *engages* listeners as *additional partners* in an already on-going 'Spirited' dialogue."[13]

Of course, if we acknowledge the communicative nature of preaching, if we approach the sermon as interaction, both listeners and preachers must take responsibility for the creation of shared meaning. In his article, "Stick it in Your Ear! Preaching as an Oral-Aural Transaction," Neil Alexander makes what he labels a "bold assertion": "People are not changed when words are spoken, but when they are heard. . . . [This] is a profound idea for the preacher to embrace."[14] And, a communication perspective would insist, a profound idea for the listener to embrace as well.

In his recent book, *The Burdensome Joy of Preaching*, acclaimed preacher James Earl Massey asks us to recall the interaction of

Jesus and his listeners: "Jesus always considered his audience, but his audience did not always rightly consider him. Both the speaker and listeners are under a mutual obligation: They should match each other in openness, purpose, and concern."[15] An impotent sermon is not a preacher's "fault." Neither is a powerful sermon's power attributable to the efforts of the preacher alone. In his magnificent but rarely cited book, *Partners in Preaching*, Reuel L. Howe concludes:

> The laymen are wrestling with the meaning of their lives and are unable to hear and understand the preaching of the church; and the preachers are struggling with the meaning of the gospel with such exclusive concentration that they are estranged from the meanings of their people. The results are obvious. There is no meeting of meaning between the preaching of the clergy and the experience of the people; and, therefore, no meeting between the Word of God and the word of man [during the sermon].[16]

Indeed, *The Great American Sermon Survey* is not an attempt to give kudos or lay blame anywhere, but rather to assert *that we're in this together.* We are communicators—as listeners and as preachers. A monologue approach minimizes the power of the spoken word to transform—leaving tuned-out listeners and stressed-out preachers. Communication is, by its very nature, a mutual endeavor.

Preachers, don't allow us listeners to be mere spectators. Listeners, you are not off the hook! Passionless sermon? Ho-hum homily? You are a partner! Several preachers in the study could recall individual listeners and groups of listeners who had invigorated their preaching. Said one, "Mrs. X was such a good listener; she fed me every moment as I preached." Said another, "Certain people pull it out of me. Their listening directs me." One Anglo-American preacher told of his first opportunity to guest-preach in an African-American church. The vocal encouragement from the listeners was incredibly heart-warming; something he had never before experienced. As he closed the sermon with his final line from his notes, one listener shouted, "You're not done yet, be-cause we're not done listening!" Luckily, he had the manuscript for his planned evening sermon to the group in the same folder so, he recalls, "I just turned the page and kept on going." Rejuvenated by his listeners' response, he spent the afternoon generating a new evening message. Listeners, we have power as partners in the in-teraction; at the very least, we have responsibility. Say preaching reformers Stanley Hauerwas and William Willimon, "There is no hearing of God's word apart from a people who are struggling to listen truthfully for God's word."[17]

## Some Communication Models

### The Linear Model

An old, linear model of communication, created by telephone com-pany workers, has been wrongfully assumed to be an appropriate model for the process of human communication for decades. This one-way model (a monologue model) represents communication as an act in which information is sent from senders, through chan-nels, to receivers.[18] The model acknowledges that there can be "noise in the channel" which distorts the intended message, but the sender-to-receiver model oversimplifies the complex process of human communication into something rather unrecognizable. Anyone who has tried to communicate with a toddler during a tem-per tantrum understands that the "receiver" has more power than this model allows.

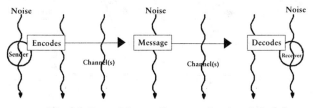

Model One: Linear Communication Model

From *Understanding Human Communication* by Ronald B. Adler and George Rodman.

A monologue model and mindset allow preaching to be treated as a "sender-to-receiver" act. The preacher plans and structures the sermon and sends it to the listeners. The listeners either receive it or they do not. This view of preaching discounts its communicative nature, diminishes its potential power, and dilutes its possible meaning. If human communication were so simple, preachers could just repeat an artful, two- or three-sentence sound byte explaining the basic gospel message again and again until we listeners "got it." This one-way model also implies that all communication is intentional, and we are well aware that preachers don't intend all the meanings listeners attribute to their behaviors. For example, listeners in this study perceive "monotone" sermons to be a sign that the preacher's life is devoid of spiritual depth or that the preacher is not sincere. Preachers know that a monotone voice could signify many other conditions, such as a hellish week that precluded adequate preparation or simply a habitual and boring speech pattern. Fortunately, we human beings are much more complex than the linear model allows.

### The Interactive Model

This "interactive" model helps us understand that differing interpretations are present in an interaction because communicators occupy different environments.

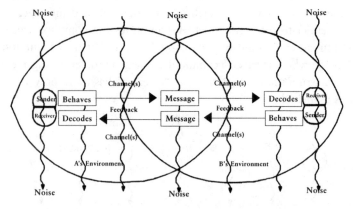

Model Two: Interactive Communication Model

From *Understanding Human Communication* by Ronald B. Adler and George Rodman.

We create meanings based on our previous experiences. Environment includes the personal experiences, the cultural background, the family setting, and even the location of a communicator.

As young teachers, my husband and I transplanted ourselves from the Midwest to a remote Alaskan village. In those classrooms on the tundra, we culturally different students and teachers tried to understand one another. My Yup'ik Eskimo students raised their eyebrows to say "yes." At first, I didn't even notice raised eyebrows; so I would ask my question again, loudly. Eyebrows would rise again. All over the room. "Yes." "Yes." "Yes." Again, I wouldn't notice.

My adolescent students asked for my assistance by demanding, "Teacher, come." It seemed rude for them to order me around, to not even say please. As that naïve teacher, I explained to my Eskimo students that my former Midwestern students requested my help by raising their hands, saying please, acting deferential. I demonstrated, the Eskimo students howled. For days, they asked for help with exaggerated syrupy politeness, followed by giggles. I finally laughed too. My former perceptions now seemed inappropriate. Together, over time, our interaction created new meanings, collaborative meanings, which we all understood. I waited for raised eyebrows after asking a question. My students began to say, "Teacher come—please," with a smile. Our shared meaning increased as a collaborative product of our interaction. Our environments overlapped.

In this example, it is easy to perceive the cultural differences, the differences in meaning created by "environment." The area of overlap in the model represents shared meanings created by common understandings or through the process of interaction. Lots of cultural difference, little shared meaning. Infrequent interaction, little shared meaning. The capacity for communicators to expand that area of shared meanings is dependent on their commitment to interaction. "We're so different, why even bother?" is an attitude that has shut down many potential relationships.

With this example in which cultural difference is so obvious, the model's meaning may be readily understood. With preaching, "environmental" and "cultural" differences may be more difficult to perceive, but they are present, let there be no doubt. The interactive model can help us determine that working to understand each other's perspectives will increase the meaning we share. Said one listener, "My preacher has no idea what my life is about. He's celibate, he lives with his head in books, he eats, drinks, and talks Scripture all day long. Sure, he's a nice guy, but when he urges me to 'give sacrificially,' I want him to understand that it's all I can do to put food on the table. He's never lived in my world."

### The Transactional Model

In this third model, communication is represented as a transaction in which participants are simultaneously "sending" and "receiving" messages.

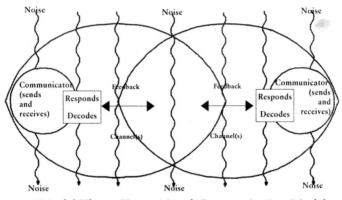

Model Three: Transactional Communication Model

From *Understanding Human Communication by Ronald B. Adler and George Rodman.*

Such a model helps us accept that communication is continuous. The transactional model also steers us away from monologue and toward dialogue, visually demonstrating that "communication isn't something we do *to* others; rather, it is an activity we do *with* them."[19]

As communicators, we simultaneously co-create meaning. In interpersonal communication, the spoken words may overlap as we interrupt, question, comment, and seek clarification. In public communication, generally one person does most of the speaking, and the other persons typically do not utter any or as many spoken words. Does this mean they are simply "receiving info" like a computer being loaded with new software? Of course not. In human communication, there are words spoken and words thought.

These processes of speech and thought are interrelated.

## Human Communication Is Unique

Human communication is interaction and transaction, continuous and mutual, unique from other forms of communication. Its power lies in the use of symbol and the connection between mind and mouth, between thought and speech. The study of speech communication is the study of the spoken word. Conceptual ability, cultural development, change, ethical considerations, and spirituality are all possible because of this uniquely human capacity. Not merely a mechanism for transferring information a little better or worse than the smoke signal or post-it-note, the spoken word rests in the uniquely human ability to use symbols.

When renowned chimpanzee researcher Jane Goodall explains the vast difference between the intellects of humans and chimpanzees, she states, "[Human intellect is possible] because we have developed a spoken language. A language which enables us to leave the present behind—we can discuss the past—we can talk about the future . . . we can pass on information to our children—because of words."[20] Communication theorist Frank E.X. Dance, in his *A Speech Theory of Human Communication* (foundational to this study), says we are different from other animals not just in degree, but in kind.[21] As my dissertation director and mentor, Dr. Dance provided a way for me and countless other scholars to philosophically defend the uniqueness of humanity. While some have called Dance's theory a "theology," its eloquence is unrivaled among those who focus their study on the spoken word. Philosopher Suzanne Langer's ideas resonate with Frank Dance's perspective. Langer's tightly reasoned arguments led to her contention that because of our ability to symbol "human nature is set apart," a "mode of being that is typified by language, culture, morality, and consciousness of life or death."[22] In *Building Communication Theory*, Dominic Infante and his co-authors assert, "Meaning is accomplished when human beings interpret symbols. Meaning is a human creation; words don't mean, people mean. That is, the meaning of symbols is provided by the people and their culture."[23]

Consequently, we can deduce that the sermon is nearly meaningless without listeners. Preachers, do you need proof? Preach your next sermon in solitude in the same sanctuary and see what happens. Yes, see what happens when the listener you know who has just lost a child is not there. When the faithful senior citizen is gone from his regular spot. When the parent whose child has come back to the faith is not seated before you. Without the listeners, there is no communication. A rehearsal to the pews can assist the preparing preacher, but the sermon gains its potential for power when the listeners arrive, when the listeners choose to use their symbolic abilities to make meaning from the spoken words.

So often we forget the very nature of the spoken word. It is easy to simply fall back on that old telephone inspired sender-to-receiver model, to think that the purpose of speech is the transfer of information. A person wants to get something from his mind to yours, so he says, "Turn the dial to the left." When monkeys want to warn their pals of a predator, they make the appropriate yelp and everybody heads for the treetops. Believing that words are merely mechanistic, rather than symbolically meaningful, shortchanges the human, perhaps even the divine.

## What Makes Human Communication Human?

Human speech is, by its nature, symbolic. Words are not things, but rather **arbitrary representations of things.** How different the monkey yelp, one of three that is instinctively and uniformly interpreted by all monkey hearers,[24] from even a simple comment like, "Turn the dial to the left!" We have to wonder who is commanding whom to turn that dial. And under what conditions? And what will happen if the dial is or is not turned? Is this dial-turning utterance from a new employee telling an experienced colleague something she already knows? From a novice daddy, trying to get his young son to turn the dial of an ignored (and developmentally inappropriate) Christmas toy? Or from a preacher exhorting his listeners to move their car radio pre-set button from their country music station to the new Christian station, reminding them that they will be able to hear his sermon for a second time bright and early on Tuesday mornings from 4:30 to 5:00?

Unlike interpreting the monkey yelp, we cannot begin to truly understand the "meaning" of an isolated human comment without being aware of some other variables like context, relationship, tone of voice, personal histories, or culture. Even with such knowledge, we cannot accurately predict the meanings the communicators will co-create. Turn the dial to the left. The experienced colleague could be pleased that the new hire knows what to do— or the words could begin a descent into a power conflict that will corrode the relationship for years. Because **symbols are arbitrary**, multiple interpretations of spoken words are always possible, indeed, are ordinary. Said a preacher from a large church in the Southeast, "My listeners seem likely to interpret the message differently than I intended." Yes, actually, multiple interpretations— different from the intended meaning—are typical.

The "mind meld" communication of the Star Trek "Vulcan" people would be a lovely development for human communicators. For those not aware of this technique, the Vulcan person simply places her hand on the mind (well, forehead) of the other and all the interior understandings of the other are vividly and completely real to the melder. The two minds literally become one. Pretty handy trick. If listeners could do the meld, we could approach our pastors and priests, place our hands on their foreheads, and have instant access to all that insight! But human communication doesn't work that way. Understanding another's mind may take years of dialogue and relationship, and even then, may never be complete. This characteristic of the spoken word can be very frustrating, yet it is the basis of our humanness, our creativity, and our uniquely human power to change and be changed.

Why this complexity of symbol interpretation? Rather than complain, we must recognize that such flexibility is precisely why the spoken word is more than a method of transferring bits of data. You see, speech and thought are related for humans. Russian psychologist L.S. Vygotsky said that to study speech and thought separately is like separately studying oxygen and hydrogen to gain an understanding of water.[25] Next time you ask, "How could he have twisted my words so much?" or "How in the world did she get that out of the homily?" remember Vygotsky's metaphor. Speech and thought are as intricately interwoven as the hydrogen and oxygen gases that combine to create that thirst quencher upon which our lives depend.

We can think of speech and thought as external and internal spoken language. Our internal words move faster than our external words. Internally, we can think from 400–4000 words per minute; externally, our average rate is around 150 words per minute.[26] There's no way preachers can talk fast enough to use all our thoughts. What are listeners doing with all those extra words per minute when they listen to a sermon? Recall a silent moment on a car trip after which you asked the other, "What are you thinking about?" While the silence may have lasted five minutes, the explanation may have taken twenty-five. Not only is thought accelerated, its grammar is condensed: "Thirsty—juice," and our legs start moving to the refrigerator. Additionally, in thought, each word is loaded with meaning; semantics are condensed. We don't find ourselves thinking, "Now, what do I mean by that?" When we think "mother" that word's meaning includes our memory of every interaction we ever had with our mothers, how we feel about becoming a mother, or about the mother of our children, etc. When used in interaction with others, the word "mother" will either be interpreted through a common, minimal definition, or the other communicators will attach their own meanings to the word we've chosen. We can't just say words and expect that they will be interpreted precisely as we use them in our own minds or precisely as we intend them. And yet many of us do have just such an expectation.

The sermon surveys show that preachers aim for clarity, but listeners complain of repetition and redundancy. Says the preacher, "My constant goal is relevancy." Says his listener, "I keep hoping for relevance. This preacher just doesn't get it." Do you remember when the famous football-playing preacher Reggie White spoke outside his pulpit and some listeners labeled him as a stereotyping, homophobic racist? Such an interpretation is certainly not what Pastor Reggie intended! And what is our response to such "misunderstanding"? Most often, we blame our listener, the human being with whom we are interacting, for not flawlessly discerning our intended meaning. We expect the mind meld; we get mental mush.

To really understand speech, we must study the mind and the spoken word simultaneously. And we must study not just the mind of the speaker but of all participants in the interaction because together they co-create meaning. Any study of spoken language which does not acknowledge the symbolic processes at work in the mind of all participants shortchanges the power of the spoken word, simplifying its very nature into something wholly unrecognizable. **Listeners and their preachers need to consider themselves partners in communication.** If we only talk about preachers and their words, we limit our understanding. This study approaches the human communication act called preaching as interaction, as the co-creation of meaning between preacher and their listeners.

While crafting meaning, carefully, conscientiously, alone in a quiet study, most preachers have the best of intentions. They may pore over commentaries, Internet sites, and multiple versions of their Biblical text, but have they studied the minds of their specific listeners? In *The Speaker's Handbook*, communication scholars Sprague and Stuart proclaim:

> A speech is not an intention in the mind of a speaker nor is it a text that exists in a vacuum. Speakers do not give speeches to audiences, they jointly create meaning with audiences. The ultimate outcome of any speech situation is a product of what the speaker actually says and how the listeners process and interpret what is said.[27]

What I have been saying is this: Preachers and listeners need to become acutely aware of the interactive nature of human communication to maximize the power of the spoken word in the preaching event. The spoken word is so potentially powerful. We diminish the power of the spoken word if we do not embrace its interactive nature. Making meaning is a mutual responsibility. From mind to mind by way of the spoken word. *We're in this together.*

## Notes

[1] Trenholm, S. (1995). *Thinking through communication: An introduction to the study of human communication.* Boston: Allyn & Bacon, 5.

[2] See Trenholm, 26.

[3] Masterson, J.T., Beebe, S.A., & Watson, N.H. (1983). *Speech communication: Theory and practice.* New York: Holt, Rinehart, and Winston, 5.

[4] See Trenholm, 26.

[5] See Masterson, 5.

[6] Dance, F.E.X., & Zak-Dance, C. (1994). *Speaking your mind: Private thinking and public speech.* Dubuque, IA: Kendall-Hunt Publishing Company, 3–23.

[7] Bull, P., & Ducat, V. (Producers and Directors). (1988). *Mind: (Episode Seven—Language)* [Video]. New York: WNET.

[8] See Trenholm, 26.

[9] Watzlawick, P. (1976). *How real is real? Confusion, disinformation, communication.* New York: Vintage Books.

[10] Duduit, M. (1999). "Preaching to the unchurched: An interview with James Emory White," *Preaching,* 14 (4), 19.

[11] McCourt, F. (1998, December). "When you think of God, what do you see?" *Life,* 63–73.

[12] Hughes, R.G., & Kysar, R. (1997). *Preaching doctrine for the twenty-first century.* Minneapolis: Fortress Press, 19.

[13] Alling, R., & Schlafer, D.J. (Eds.). (1997). *Preaching as the art of sacred conversation: Sermons that work VI.* Harrisburg, PA: Morehouse Publishing, xi.

[14] Alexander, N. (1998). "Stick it in your ear! Preaching as an oral-aural transaction." In R. Alling and D.J. Schlafer (Eds.), *Preaching as image and story and idea: Sermons that work VII* (pp. 35–40). Harrisburg, PA: Morehouse Publishing.

[15] Massey, J.E. (1998). *The burdensome joy of preaching.* Nashville, TN: Abingdon Press, 57.

[16] Howe, R.L. (1967). *Partners in preaching: Clergy and laity in dialogue.* New York: The Seabury Press, 18–19.

[17] Hauerwas, S., & Willimon, W.H. (1989). *Resident Aliens.* Nashville, TN: Abingdon Press, 128.

[18] Shannon, C.E., & Weaver, W. (1949). *The mathematical theory of communication*. Urbana, IL: University of Illinois Press.

[19] Adler, R.B., & Rodman, G. (1997). *Understanding human communication* (6th ed.). New York: Harcourt Brace College Publishers, 15–16.

[20] See Bull, & Ducat.

[21] Dance, F.E.X. (1982). "A speech theory of human communication." In F.E.X. Dance (Ed.), *Human communication theory: Comparative essays* (pp. 120–146). New York: Harper and Row. See also, Dance, F.E.X. (1973). "Speech communication: The revealing echo." In L. Thayer (Ed.), *Communication: Ethical and moral issues*. New York: Gordan and Breach.

[22] Langer, S. (1967). *Mind: An essay on human feelings (Vol. 1)*. Baltimore, MD: Johns Hopkins University Press.

[23] Infante, D., Rancer, A.S., & Womack, D.F. (1990). *Building communication theory*. Prospect Heights, IL: Waveland Press, 197.

[24] See Bull, & Ducat.

[25] Rieber, R.W., & Carton, A.S. (Eds.), (1987). *The collected works of L.S. Vygotsky*. New York: Plenum Press.

[26] See Dance, & Zak-Dance, 215–217.

[27] Sprague, J., & Stuart, D. (1996). *The speaker's handbook* (4th ed.). Fort Worth, TX: Harcourt Brace & Company, 41.

Chapter 3

# Rethink These Please

S WE CONTINUE our consideration of the power of the spoken word, let's attempt to "pass" a communication quiz. No grade! No pressure! Just follow these directions: using the following scale, place the number matching your response next to each statement:

1 = Strongly Disagree
2 = Disagree
3 = Don't Know
4 = Agree
5 = Strongly Agree

## Communication Quiz

___ Positive intentions create effective communication.

___ If preachers study communication, they will be asked to compromise Truth.

___ The phrase *communication competence* means "doing whatever works."

___ Preachers concerned with listeners' perspectives are likely to become ineffectual people-pleasers.

___ In a public speech, the speaker is responsible for the success of the speech.

___ When it comes to communication, some people are just "born gifted."

_____ Listeners are not expected to talk to the preacher about the sermon.

_____ More communication means better communication.

_____ Churches have conflict because people in the church don't communicate.

_____ Issues of culture, gender, and power do not affect church communication because we are all equal in the sight of God.

_____ If we just had more communication, everything would be better.

_____ Some preachers are just not communicators.

_____ Preachers choose each week whether to preach about the love of God or the obedience God expects.

_____ In most churches, listeners and preachers share the same background.

_____ Listeners have no power during a sermon.

_____ There is one best way for preachers to preach.

_____ A "bad sermon" occurs because the listener is not trying hard enough.

_____ If the preacher gives the listeners what they want, the sermon will be short and meaningless.

_____ Preachers don't need to study public speaking because the Holy Spirit will use their message no matter how it is organized and delivered.

_____ Communication is a good thing.

McDonald's playland is a fascinating place to conduct research. As parents let their pre-schoolers romp in a relatively safe (at least well-padded) environment, some try to read the paper or stare into space, convincing themselves that such a moment is that "time alone" everyone keeps saying they need. Invariably, this pseudo-isolation is usurped by a child needing a Kleenex or conflict mediator, the silence is broken, and the parents of various children begin to chat with each other. "Oh, mine was just like that at two. Don't worry. Three is worse." "I should buy stock in the Kleenex Corporation. My little one sniffles from October 'til March." As the discussion proceeds from diapers to dance class to divorce, the (eavesdropping) researcher, hiding behind a fresh copy of "Parents" magazine, can begin to work. It is through just such a "scientific" process of listening to everyday talk that a list of "commonly accepted ideas about communication" has been compiled. Let's inspect and consider these ideas as we continue to explore the power and nature of human communication.

Don't worry—we'll be back to the quiz soon enough.

## Myth: Communication Is "The Answer"

Walk into any bookstore in America, head to the "self-help" section, and you'll discover numerous pop-psychology books declaring that "Communication is The Answer." Back covers will promote the notion that "you just need to learn to communicate" with these "five easy steps" and your relationship problems will vanish. (Only $29.95, accompanying audio tape $59.95 with a three-day workshop coming to your area soon.)

Have you heard this comment explaining a just-revealed, impending divorce? "They just didn't communicate." Or, have you heard the constant refrain of parents of young children, tag-teaming childcare with one another, working in and out of the home round the clock: "We just don't communicate anymore." Or the senior citizen parent of a distant adult child wishing that "we had more communication."

Even one listener in this sermon survey research fantasized, "If only our preacher could learn to communicate."

If only we had: Communication. More communication. We'd have The Answer. No one wishes this kind of thinking were defensible more than the human communication professors themselves. If only our discipline could be The Answer. If only doing *more* of our subject matter could alleviate the pain of relationship problems altogether. Whether motivated by an intense desire to make a difference in the world or by the fame, wealth, and early retirement available to those who provide panaceas, we'd certainly be in greater demand than we currently find ourselves! But, (especially) those of us who study the powerful spoken word must be the first to admit that a "lack of communication" is not the problem and therefore, "more communication" cannot be The Answer.

"Why not?" someone challenges.

First, let's refer to one of our definitions of human communication from Chapter Two: "Human communication is a process whereby people assign meanings to stimuli in order to make sense of the world."[1]

When we use our minds to make meaning of the words or behavior of others, communication has occurred. Communication is continuous. To use some poor grammar: We cannot not communicate. Some of my college students studying communication have proposed some marvelous challenges to this notion; for example, "What if I'm spelunking alone and get lost in a cave, and fall, hitting my head so hard that I go into a coma . . . am I still communicating?"

So, we might want to qualify the statement: When in the presence of an observing, conscious human being, you cannot not communicate. Try it. Right now. Find a person or two. Tell them you want to "not communicate" to them for a full thirty seconds. What happened? Laughter? Silence? Turning away? Ask them what meanings they made from your behavior. Silly? Snobby? Snide? You communicated. You couldn't help it. "Because communication is nonverbal as well as verbal, we are always sending behavioral messages from which others draw inferences or meaning," says Distinguished Teaching Professor of Communication, Rudolph Verderber.[2] When another person gives meaning to your behavior, you have communicated.

Let's consider that divorce being dissected at the McDonald's playland—and the summative diagnosis: "They just didn't communicate." Well, for a divorce proceeding to be on the court schedule, communication has occurred. Screaming battles before bed, communicating anger and disrespect. No expressions of care, communicating indifference. Trust-breaking behaviors, communicating that "promises made are no longer to be kept." A chilly silence, communicating, "It's not even worth talking about this anymore" or "that subject is now taboo."

Yes, we even make meanings from the silence of others. We don't stop communicating because we stop talking. Remember Vygotsky's hydrogen and oxygen analogy about the relationship of mind and mouth? As long as we're using words to make meanings in our minds, communication is occurring. Legal papers served, communicating, "I really mean it. I don't love you anymore. I don't want to grow old with you. It's over." Lack of communication? To the contrary, communication is most definitely occurring. Meanings are co-created, interactants are affected.

Of course, sometimes, silence is a way to communicate great compassion and deep understanding. Choosing not to speak the phrase, "I told you so," when you might be correct in such an assessment. Choosing not to speak, but just to *be* in the presence of a grieving friend, when any utterance would be inadequate for the depth of despair. Silence communicates, and the more well known the communication partner, the more shared meanings are created from the quiet interludes. In one study of couples happily married fifty years or more, communication researcher Judith Pearson uncovered a surprising result. After couples had been identified as "happily married" by each spouse and several family members and friends, they were interviewed regarding the communication in their relationship. Not only did long-term, happily married spouses interrupt and finish each other's sentences, many of the couples revealed that silence about certain topics was a part of their marital communication pattern. Mind you, this is not the silence of taboo topics chilled before the first anniversary, but the respectful, compassionate silence of grief already processed, or wounds, long since forgiven and "forgotten," never to be dredged up again.[3]

Since not all relationships are so long-term and healthy as to allow "shared meaning" in silence, silence can be a confusing component of communication. One finding of *The Great American Sermon Survey* shows that it is extremely rare for preachers and listeners to talk about the content of sermons. Silence about the meaning of the sermon (or the near silence of trite, repetitive remarks) seems to be common in many (but not all) churches. "A process for that kind of dialogue just doesn't exist," says a listener from the Southwest. "I'm really not sure my personality could take the negative feedback if I initiated such a process," admits a preacher from the West. Does this silence between listener and preacher communicate anything? Of course. But what? The meanings are diverse. Many listeners say, "If there's ever anything wrong, I'll let the preacher know." (Sounds a little like the husband who said, "I told you I loved you seventeen years ago on our wedding day. If anything changes, I'll be sure to let you know.") Other listeners say, "I always make a comment when the sermon is good." If the silence of some listeners is intended to mean, "It *wasn't* a good sermon" and the silence of others is planned to communicate "It *was* a good sermon" what meaning will the preacher give to the silence, and to the comments?

The silence can and will be interpreted in a variety of ways. Says one preacher, "As long as I don't hear anything, I know I'm okay. I dread those Monday morning phone calls, because they usually mean somebody is mad." While another preacher counters, "The silence is deafening. I can be thinking 'I'm God's gift to preaching' and maybe the quiet guy in the corner is considering suggesting a career change for me." Yet another preacher relishes "the sort of silence that lets you know they are in the palm of your hand." It's not that communication is lacking, for silence communicates; rather, it is the *ambiguous* nature of silence; the lack of shared meaning about the silence, that we must scrutinize.

## Myth: Communication Is a Good Thing

Another myth that often accompanies this "More communication is the remedy" mentality, is the "Communication is always a good thing" concept. This book asserts that human communication is potentially powerful, but not that it is inherently good. "In truth," remind communication professors Adler and Rodman, "Communication is neither good nor bad in itself. Rather, its value comes from the way it is used."[4] Think of fire, burning brightly in a stone fireplace, casting a glow on long-married lovers reminiscing about winters now past. Or fire, creating life-giving warmth to hikers lost in the mountains during a surprise spring snowstorm. Then remember ferocious flames consuming an upstairs apartment on a cold Christmas Eve, stealing life and belongings. The power for good or evil is in the purpose and the impact, not in the fire itself. And what about salt? A bit of seasoning for your baked potato or a blood pressure pumper-upper? Have you grabbed a cookie only to discern with the first unsettling bite that someone substituted salt for sugar? How we use something determines the outcome.

**Like most all gifts given to humans, the spoken word has the potential to be used for good or for evil, or even to be wasted on mediocrity.** Theorists Frank Dance and Carol Zak-Dance focus our attention on a well-known, deplorable use of the spoken word to communicate—powerfully.

> Adolph Hitler testified in print and in speech that he considered the spoken word his most powerful weapon. Using the spoken word, Hitler rose from obscurity to become the chancellor of Germany. Using the spoken word—in fact insisting that his personal spoken word be accepted as the law of the land—Hitler talked more than 12 million human beings into their graves. Using the spoken word, Hitler destroyed the interior balance of his own subjects so that among those followers some turned themselves from normal human beings into malicious and almost bestial predators. Hitler and his minister of propaganda, Joseph Goebbels, exemplify the power of the spoken word used on behalf of an inhumane ethic.[5]

Remember the film titled *The Apostle*? The lead character, a preacher with haunting sins of his own, in a matter of moments was able to use spoken words to transform an angry, violent bulldozer driver, intent on smashing the church building, into a repentant, gentle, tearful believer.

Said a listener in this sermon study, "Becoming a widow was extremely hard for me to adjust to and I became very depressed. Then, one Sunday, my pastor preached on 'How to Cope After Losing a Loved One.' It seemed he was preaching to me and I grasped every word and it helped set me free." Several preachers could recall words spoken by listeners regarding the impact of a particular sermon on their lives; for example, "You saved my life, Preacher. I just want you to know, that sermon saved my life."

Those words continue to serve as an encouraging memory in the mind of the preacher who heard them.

Is communication potentially powerful? We better understand the affirmative answer to that question and take it seriously. Carelessness with our words and our silences is perhaps such a common phenomenon that we forget that flame, that salt, that power of human communication. The power of human communication is a potential, waiting to be used. We don't need more talk or more action; we're already communicating every time we're in the presence of another human being. It's the *quality* of our communication, not the quantity, which we need to consider.

## Myth: Good Communicators Are Born, Not Made

After the artful telling of a relevant, humorous story presented from multiple perspectives using language in such a way as to evoke concrete visual images, the preacher spends the last moments of the sermon repeating two key words from the Scripture reading, and closes by asking one thought provoking, key-idea question for the listeners to consider during the week. (You can bet that sermon had no sentences as lengthy as the one you just completed!) The air is electric during the sermon as listeners rivet their attention on the story, the Scripture, and the "So what?" question. As the sermon concludes, the last teary eye is wiped, and the final hand shaken, the meanings given to that preacher's words *affect* many of those who have heard.

In fact, would you believe it, two of those listeners even chatted about answers to that application question as they passed time in the (aforementioned) playland. Yes, they really did! And when they were done brainstorming responses, one of them remarked, "Isn't the preacher an incredibility gifted communicator? Some people are so lucky to be born with great communication skills. I can hardly introduce myself at a Pampered Chef party, let alone give a meaningful public presentation like a sermon!"

Born with it? Really? Probably, that preacher wouldn't have liked the "gifted communicator" label, wanting his listeners to focus on the message rather than on the messenger. Most preachers interviewed for this study disclose such an attitude. Says one preacher from a large parish, "I'm never satisfied with a 'good sermon' remark. I ask them what part of the message was meaningful to them."

But some non-preachers who have been called "gifted" and "born with it" reveal that they dislike such comments for another reason. Why? The "born with a gift" label can imply that whatever ability they are displaying was not learned, did not take practice, and was present on the day of their birth. Since genetic potential for spoken language is present in the developing infant, we tend to mistakenly think the *way* we use spoken language is also "just natural." Says communication textbook author Rudy Verderber,

> Because of our background, each of us has some of the communication skills we need to be effective in our dealings with others. However, we also lack some of the skills we need. As a result, each of us can benefit from continuous learning and skill practice.[6]

## Human Communication is Learned

Whether at the knee of a story-telling grandpa, or in a household where silence brings fear, or from a teacher who validated our long-winded answers or in a high school speech class, our use of spoken language has been *learned*. Rather than assuming that some are *born* "good communicators" and some are not, we all—preachers and listeners—need to recognize that learning to *use* spoken language internally and externally began in childhood and continues for the duration of our existence.

Are these innate gifts, or predisposed potentials waiting for our effort to awaken them? Howard Gardner postulates that traditional IQ scores are inadequate for explaining the excellence of people in certain arenas of life. He talks about the potential for certain intelligences (including linguistic, musical, logical-mathematical, spatial, bodily-kinesthetic, and interpersonal intelligences) being greatly influenced by life experiences.[7] While some of us may have developed interpersonal intelligence rather than musical intelligence, the "gift" of the spoken word is a potential given to almost all humans. **Accepting our current communication competence level as innate is detrimental thinking.**

Rather than framing the discussion of human communication as "You have The Gift" or "You don't have The Gift," it will be much more helpful to broaden our understanding of communication to discussions of *degrees of communication competence* in various contexts. Excusing mediocrity with an "I just wasn't born a gifted communicator" would be a false extension of the assumption under consideration. Poor listening behaviors? What has been learned can be unlearned. Adequate but not consistently transformational sermons? Further learning can enhance competence, or grow it in new directions. Though there are numerous excellent preachers and listeners, probably not too many of us are ready for a rest stop on our quest for higher levels of communication competence.

## Myth: Competent Communicators Get What They Want

What is human communication competence? First, we have to debunk this common perception that competence means only "effectiveness"—that is, "getting what you want from the other person." If such a limiting definition is used, then Jerry Springer and Hitler and an abusive parent could all be ranked as "highly competent communicators." Not so. Communication competence must include an "appropriateness" element that takes into consideration the ethics of the context of human communication as well as the needs and goals of all participants.[8]

Communication competence develops in many ways. Competent sermon communicators will develop a heightened awareness of their own behavior[9] as well as an awareness of the perspective of their communication partner. Indeed, empathy has been found to be a central component of communication competence.[10] Competent preachers will have the sensitivity and skill to change direction during the interaction if listener responses call for such change. Importantly, commitment to the relationship with the interaction partner is imperative for those wishing to improve their communication competency.[11] And finally, sermon interaction must happen in such a way that participants in the interaction co-create shared meaning and are satisfied with the effect on each other.[12]

Most of us have room for continued growth in the arena of human communication competence. At the very least, you may be becoming a little more convinced that human communication competence is *learned* rather than distributed only to certain lucky folks.

## Myth: There Is One Best Way to Communicate

Along with the habit of explaining high degrees of communication competence as an innate gift can come the faulty assumption that there is one best way to communicate in relationships, in teaching, and even in preaching. In other words, one method that is "communication competence personified." Stuart Briscoe was the name of a preacher that a listener praises as "The Model" of preaching excellence. She says, "I want my preacher to be like Stuart Briscoe. I want a preacher who can take a verse and be able to speak thirty minutes on that verse in an original, applicable, relevant way—with insight—something I would never think of, deep and meaningful." While Briscoe's style has had great impact, it is not the only, or The Best, style of highly competent preaching communication. It may actually be The Best for a certain type of listener, but probably not for all.

Various types of preaching have been promoted as The Best, or The Most Spiritual over the years, including "expository preaching." Some preachers have defended this type of preaching as more spiritual than storytelling, inductive reasoning, or other non-linear organizational patterns. Another view is offered by well-known conservative Christian preacher and thinker John W. Stott:

> If by expository sermon is meant a verse-by-verse explanation of a lengthy passage of Scripture, then indeed it is only one possible way of preaching, but this would be a misuse of the word . . . To expound Scripture is to bring out of the text what is there and expose it to view.[13]

With this definition of expository preaching, many more organizational (and even delivery) options are available to those who align themselves with the "expository method." Stephen Farris, author of *Preaching That Matters*, joins the discussion with his assertion that

> Preaching may be recognized as the word of God
> when it coheres with the biblical witness. Nor-
> mally this will mean that the sermon will grow
> from our interaction with a biblical text. There
> are, however, textual sermons that are profoundly
> unbiblical and non-textual sermons that are truly
> biblical.[14]

Since the Christian message is supposed to be for all people in all cultures at all moments of history, a variety of methods of preaching the message would seem necessary and defensible.

Even those who do find a style of preaching that feels "right" to them, cannot assume that it is the best, the most effective, for others in other contexts or for every listener in a given church. Take a moment to recall Martin Luther King, Jr.'s sermons. His style had tremendous transformational impact, but that doesn't mean that a Korean preacher on the West Coast, presenting sermons to third-generation Korean-Americans, should adopt King's style!

Some preachers in this study mention that listeners have an idealized image of The Right Way to preach, often a caricature of a former preacher, through which the current preacher is continually evaluated. In the book, *Pastor to Pastor*, author Erwin Lutzer suggests, "If ten pastors preached the same message verbatim, the results would not be the same. Some pastors exude instant charisma; others are more yielded to the Spirit or have greater gifts. It's not just what is said but who says it that makes a difference."[15] After reading the previous chapters, perhaps you are ready to add to Lutzer's comment—not only who *says* it but also who *is listening* can make a startling difference. What is "highly competent preaching" for one group of listeners in a particular church will likely not be as highly competent in another setting. Moving toward the destination of communication competence will be a different journey for each of us. Looking for a magic model is less helpful than looking to a personal discovery of higher degrees of competence in a particular context with specific partners in communication.

## Myth: In Good Communication, Content Is Everything

Since commitment to the relationship is a component of competence, this journey toward sermon competence can be further enhanced if we remember that communication has both content *and* relational dimensions.[16] Says a listener when giving advice to preachers, "If they would treat all people the same. I realize that each of us have people we like and enjoy more than others. But I feel if you checked into whom the preacher visits over a period of several years there is a definite pattern. I have been an active member of my church for 30 years and have had only two ministers who have ever come to visit. None ever came for family deaths and illnesses . . . other hurt members often feel neglected and because of that separate themselves from the Christian body."

We don't know if this listener talked to her preachers or not. Let's hypothesize for a minute that she did not; but rather, that she has assumed her preachers should know her expectation and is offended that they didn't. Not just offended, but hurt, as she perceives their actions as a lack of caring, a relationship slight. And that perceived lack of caring no doubt serves as a filtering device when she listens to her current preacher preach.

One preacher tells of his experiences in a middle-class farming community, describing his quiet congregation, and their lack of verbal feedback. "I was visiting a parishioner whose daughter from out of town—who'd heard last Sunday's sermon—had told her folks how wonderful the sermon was. As the mother began to tell me what the daughter had said, her husband 'shushed' her, whispering, 'Don't tell him that. He's going to want a raise.'"

While it's rare for listeners and preachers to speak directly and deeply about the content of a sermon, another kind of talk is rarer still. J.A. Sparks, author of *Pot-shots at the Preacher,* claims that "the issue that clergy and congregation seem most to avoid is straight talk about their relationship."[17] "Relationship talk is being open, direct, and present to the other, reading into the other person's world without giving up your own, to look at your common experiences from the other's standpoint."[18]

In the absence of direct relationship talk—meanings about the relationship are still communicated, though primarily through actions (like visiting or not visiting) and *how* we say what we say rather than in simply *what* we say. Even the statement, "I forgive you," can communicate negative relationship messages. Try saying this "I forgive you" phrase in ways that communicate the following:

(1)    I don't forgive you at all.

(2)    You need forgiveness even though you refuse to apologize.

(3)    You better forgive me too.

(4)    Our relationship is over.

How'd it go? Such complex relational messages can become shared meaning, relational meaning, without direct relationship talk!

Becoming aware of the content and relational dimensions of human communication is necessary for those pursuing a greater degree of communication competence.[19] Sermon *delivery* then becomes important as preachers, standing in the role of "God's Messengers," communicate not only some important content, but also the relationship that God wants to have with the listeners. Pastor Erwin Lutzer suggests to preachers that they be about the business of "genuinely loving our people" because "information alone will not change their attitudes and behavior."[20] Says a preacher in this study, "In one of the best sermons I ever heard, the preacher said, 'You can't just go around telling people not to do wrong—show them love, teach them to love, and the love will push out the wrong.'" Seventeen percent of the surveyed listeners agree that the one message they want to get across to all preachers in the United States is the importance of a loving relationship between preacher and listeners: "Work on your relationship with your listeners. Get to know us. Show us you love us. Model God's love for us as you preach." An interviewed preacher concurs, "You have to maintain a relationship during preaching or you may as well pass out a manuscript for everyone to read."

Working toward higher degrees of communication competence during sermon time will hopefully become a goal of many listeners and preachers who read this book. If "giftedness" can be perceived as a potential for using spoken language for positive, spiritual transformation, then indeed, we all have such a potential. Some preachers seem to have developed their public speaking potential in ways that are quite meaningful to their listeners; we tend to perceive such preachers as "gifted"—but we must recognize that such giftedness is a product of both potential and acquired skill.

Preacher Ed Rowell reflects, "Those gifted at communication always live with the nagging suspicion that they can get along pretty good without spiritual depth; the spiritually sensitive may believe they can be effective without good communication skills. Neither are true, and both inevitably hurt both preachers and congregation."[21]

Yes, the consideration of communication competence leads us logically to questions of ethics. Listeners undoubtedly are concerned with the ethics of preacher communication: "Do their spiritual lives correspond with what they preach?" is a question posed in one way or another by another 17 percent of the listeners in this study.

## Myth: Communication Competence Is Essentially Non-Spiritual Behavior

While all preachers must continually be aware of the ethical dilemmas of their preaching task, there are a few preachers who are skimming through a borrowed copy of this book, wary of the viewpoint of an academic in the discipline of speech communication. Their ideas about communication are never overheard in the McDonald's context, but are familiar to many who prepare sermons. While a large majority of the preachers participating in this study did not reveal the following attitudes, a few did, and several of those who chose *not* to participate in the study made statements like this . . .

- "Considering communication can easily lead to compromising Truth."
- "Because our message is so compelling, and our intentions are positive, we don't need to think about public speaking 'tricks.'"

- "Sermons are so unique from other forms of human communication that general communication principles just don't apply."
- "The Holy Spirit makes consideration of communication competence unnecessary."
- "Considering listeners' viewpoints will turn the preacher into a pandering, impotent, paranoid people-pleaser."

Protestant preacher Stephen Olford's 1998 book, *Anointed Expository Preaching*, was declared "Book of the Year" by *Preaching* magazine. Highly regarded in conservative preaching circles, Olford and his son David, who assisted with the book, thoroughly examine preaching using a careful method of scriptural analysis. The standards for appropriate, Biblically based, sermon communication delineated by the Olfords are "truth, clarity, and passion."[22] Those three foundational concepts are mentioned over and over in the book, as standards preachers should use to evaluate their own sermons. Preachers (or listeners!) who hold to ideas like "Communication techniques are unethical" are invited to process everything else in this book through the sieve of the Olfords' three standards: Truth, Clarity, and Passion—Biblically founded criteria of sermon communication competence.

### Myth: The Listeners' Perspectives of the Sermon Are Irrelevant

Human communication scholars add to "The Sieve" of truth, clarity, and passion, what we would consider The Vital Piece of the communication puzzle: the listener as partner in the interaction of the sermon. Be sure to note, however, that it was a preacher, not a communication researcher, who first titled a book with the phrase "Partners in Preaching."[23] A thoughtful preacher from the Northeast explains the sense of caution he feels, "I don't want to be so listener-focused that I end up compromising the message, but I have to know where people are."

Underlying the concern that taking listeners' perspectives into account might lead to "pandering" is a deeper assumption that what listeners want from a sermon is something less than they *should want* or something less than what the preacher thinks they need to hear. For example, a preacher might make a generalization from an idea such as the one posed by Neil Postman in *Amusing Ourselves to Death*,[24] and begin to assume that sermon listeners just want to be amused or that preachers of large churches are "simply in the entertainment business." Of course, we all appreciate a bit of well-placed humor, but asked why they listen to sermons, only one listener in the study replied "entertainment." As one preacher says, "What does a listener want from a sermon? Probably they say we should just tell them to go ahead and sin if it makes them happy." Not even one of nearly 500 listeners in this study made a comment that was remotely akin to the above statement. Preachers, if you're cautious about being accommodating to listeners' wants and needs, please process the "Listeners' Leanings" chapter carefully, using your sieve of truth, clarity, and passion.

Many listeners mention the vitality and meaningfulness of the children's sermon in their own lives. Such sermons often use a concrete object as metaphor for a key spiritual idea, vocabulary tailored to the children's developmental level, and a direct application of the spiritual concept to the daily lives of the children. Children also may expect to be partners in communication at church. A preacher from the East Coast tells about her Saturday night church service. "Because there were lots of children listening, and no children's sermon on Saturday night, I was purposefully more explanatory in that service. The children got into the habit of stopping me in the middle of the sermon to ask, 'What is this or that?' I got used to it, learned it was okay for Saturday night. Now, when some of those Saturday night children attend the Sunday service and I ask a rhetorical question, a kid's hand will go up. I love it."

How is it that most of us can appreciate accommodation of a sermon to a child's perspective, but not all of us are comfortable with "accommodation" to adult perspectives? Hauerwas and Willimon caution preachers against accommodating the hearers by "trying to make the sermon fit their established habits of understanding, which only underwrites the further political accommodation of the church to the status quo."[25] Yet L.T. Tisdale reminds us that Calvin speaks of "accommodation" as "being a part of God's gracious divine action through which God takes the initiative and rhetorically bridges—through word and deed—the great gulf that exists between human beings and God."[26]

Diluting the message by pandering to listeners' biases is quite a different matter than wanting to connect the sermon to the lives of a particular group of listening human beings. When I teach students in my "Intercultural Communication" course, my goal is to challenge them to seek and appreciate cultural viewpoints that differ from their own. Many are reluctant. Some are suspicious. No matter what, I must find a way to connect to where they are if I am to have any chance of leading them somewhere else.

Sermons can be scripturally based *and* relevant. In fact, the listeners in this study overwhelmingly request *that* specific combination. We can have both depth and connection—indeed, we must. One listener explains the relevancy he so desires, and uses the ministry of Jesus as justification: "Jesus met people where they were." An interviewed preacher proclaims, "Jesus was always very needs based. He balanced the two needs at the same time. The needs of the Father and the people. If you are not preaching to where people are with the goal of bringing them to God, you are not doing your job."

Do unethical communication strategies exist? Of course. Do respected scholars of human communication develop and promote such strategies, or do they ignore the matter of ethics when they teach about the spoken word? Absolutely not. Frank Dance explains at length how the spoken word creates the possibility for ethical considerations in the first place.[27] Rudolph Verderber,[28] Ronald Adler and George Rodman,[29] Sarah Trenholm,[30] and other authors of widely used introductory communication texts promote ethical considerations as integral components to acting out and reflecting upon the pursuit of human communication competence. Sure, those pop-psychology "Communication Is The Answer" books might describe a way to manipulate the emotions of others so you can get what you want, but such approaches are not central, nor are they celebrated, within the academic community.

We identified in Chapter One what makes the sermon a unique

form of face-to-face public communication: demand for extremely high credibility, the preacher as God's Messenger, and Scripture as the foundation. Do these unique characteristics cause general human communication principles to be non-applicable to the sermon?

One preacher who declined to be a part of this study explains: "The sermon is not human communication at all, but divine communication. Our business is proclamation. Just say the Truth of the gospel, don't try to persuade. Leave persuasion up to the Holy Spirit." Obviously, the Holy Spirit's work is hardly a subject for a communication researcher to attempt to explain.

Preachers interviewed in this study, however, describe the work of the Holy Spirit and some use phrases like "readiness" of both preachers and listeners, as well as a profound spiritual "meaningfulness" generated in the minds of the listeners during and after the sermon. Others describe examples of "fortuitous timing" (such as when a preacher did not know the circumstance of a specific listener, but spoke right to her pain) and uncanny strength to preach after an especially difficult week. The interviewed preachers did not describe the Holy Spirit as some sort of Magic Genie whose customary methodology is to absolve humans of responsibility for their spiritual lives. Preachers in this study did not suggest that we quote a verse about God's protection and then walk in front of a bus, relying on the Holy Spirit.

A careful reading of Olford's work shows that he would *not* support beliefs about the Holy Spirit's work being used to defend obtuse organizational patterns, irrelevant illustrations, monotone manuscript reading, lack of rehearsal, routine mediocrity, or derailing tangents. Please consider the following respectfully submitted perception: The Holy Spirit enhances the efforts of communicators in the church context, but the Holy Spirit is not to be used as an excuse for any lack of effort on our part.

As the nun character in the film *Sister Act*, Whoopi Goldberg justifies her radical shift to a (way) "up tempo" musical style for the church services by saying that her kind of music will "get more butts in the seats!" Of course, many real nuns would not use that particular vocabulary word for the gluteus maximus, but many nuns, priests, and pastors do consider how to connect with the culture of their listeners. From a communication perspective, the goal is not *more* people (more seats in the seats)—or *more* communication—but rather, more co-created shared meaning with discernible, positive, powerful consequences.

Now, if you don't mind, would you please take this quiz again without referring back to your previous answers? Then find a listener or preacher with whom to discuss your answers to both the pre- and post-tests. Maybe you could go out to eat at your favorite fast food playland for this little chat . . . you never know who might be listening.

Directions: Using the following scale, place the number matching your response next to each statement.

1  = Strongly Disagree
2  = Disagree
3  = Don't Know
4  = Agree
5  = Strongly Agree

## Communication Quiz

____ Positive intentions create effective communication.

____ If preachers study communication, they will be asked to compromise Truth.

____ The phrase *communication competence* means "doing whatever works."

____ Preachers concerned with listeners' perspectives are likely to become ineffectual people-pleasers.

____ In a public speech, the speaker is responsible for the success of the speech.

____ When it comes to communication, some people are just "born gifted."

____ Listeners are not expected to talk to the preacher about the sermon.

____ More communication means better communication.

____ Churches have conflict because people in the church don't communicate.

_____ Issues of culture, gender, and power do not affect church communication because we are all equal in the sight of God.

_____ If we just had more communication, everything would be better.

_____ Some preachers are just not communicators.

_____ Preachers choose each week whether to preach about the love of God or the obedience God expects.

_____ In most churches, listeners and preachers share the same background.

_____ Listeners have no power during a sermon.

_____ There is one best way for preachers to preach.

_____ A "bad sermon" occurs because the listener is not trying hard enough.

_____ If the preacher gives the listeners what they want, the sermon will be short and meaningless.

_____ Preachers don't need to study public speaking because the Holy Spirit will use their message no matter how it is organized and delivered.

_____ Communication is a good thing.

## Myth: Words Don't Have Much Power

In this first section of the book, you've been asked to become reflective about human communication. Rather than perceiving it as simply a mechanism for transferring information to "receivers," you may now be recognizing that not only are we "in this together" as listeners and preachers, we are also involved in a potentially powerful interaction.

As we rethink communication concepts, please consider this final precept: Human communication cannot be erased. It is irreversible. While some imagine spoken words as evaporating a nanosecond after utterance, the spoken word can actively survive in the minds of others for the rest of their lives. If you've said something and immediately wished you could retract it, you understand this communication principle. No amount of back-tracking and denial can erase the meanings already made. There is no delete button once words have moved from mind through mouth to another mind. While many spoken words are indeed forgotten, many other spoken words are lasting. Words spoken in the sermon have such potential. As you get ready to examine one another's perceptions of the sermon in Section Two, remember the words of life-long communication scholars, Dance and Zak-Dance, "This uniquely human ability to use spoken language to communicate gives humans additional and unusual power."[31]

Spoken words. Powerful, uniquely human utterances constructed through symbolic conceptual abilities, given meaning in interaction.

- "I've never been so disappointed with anyone in my whole life."
- "Will you marry me?"
- "From this day on, I no longer have a son."
- "God loves you. Profoundly. Constantly. Eternally."
- "I forgive you."
- "I'm sorry. We couldn't save your father."
- "Let's adopt a baby."
- "While I'd like to be able to say that suicide is forgivable, I cannot offer you that comfort at this time of grief. The Bible is clear on this issue; hell is the punishment." —a listener's recollection of a preacher's post-funeral sermon

Yes, words can change moments; words can change lives. A word, spoken in a specific instance, to another human being can maim, heal, scar, destroy, or restore.

Imagine an instance in *your* past. Words spoken carelessly or deliberately. Words that you gave meaning that will echo through the corridors of your being forever. One thirty-something woman is haunted by a comment crudely spouted from the mouth of a college classmate: "Boy, you are the only person I know who can look so good with makeup and look so ugly without it." Careless. Stupid. Unnecessary words. Yet the listening human mind makes meaning and has memory.

Do you remember such words from a teacher?

- "This artwork is truly creative."
- "Good morning, future garbage men of America."
- "You have been gifted with a fine mind."
- "Wrong again."

Such words spoken once—or routinely—from a respected (or detested) teacher may affect your perceptions of self to this very day. Whether you rebelled to prove the "garbage men" greeter wrong or devoted hundreds of hours to the enjoyment and exploration of your artistic soul, the spoken words made a lasting impression.

Can you recall these words spoken by a public figure to untold numbers of listeners?

- "I have a dream." –Martin Luther King, Jr.
- "I have ploughed, and planted, and gathered into barns. . . And a'n't I a woman? I have borne thirteen chilern, and seen 'em mos' all sold off to slavery, and when I cried out with my mother's grief, none but Jesus heard me! An a'n't I a woman?" –Sojourner Truth[32]
- "We shall fight on the beaches, we shall fight on the landing grounds, we shall fight in the fields and in the streets, we shall fight in the hills; we shall never surrender." – Winston Churchill (after the battle of Dunkirk)
- "Ask not what your country can do for you; ask what you can do for your country." –John F. Kennedy
- "I did not have 'sexual relations' with that woman." –Bill Clinton

The spoken word has impact. Permanent reverberations. One of the preachers participating in this study remarked, "We'd better be nervous. We are talking about serious stuff. If we don't do it right, it can affect somebody's soul." The potential power of the spoken word must be understood by both listeners and their preachers in this communicative event we call "sermon."

## Notes

[1] Trenholm, S. (1995). *Thinking through communication: An introduction to the study of human communication.* Boston: Allyn & Bacon, 5.

[2] Verderber, R, (1996). *Communicate!* (8th ed.). Belmont, CA: Wadsworth, 16.

[3] Pearson, J.C. (1991, January). "Communication characteristics of long-term, happily married couples." Research summary presented to graduate students at the University of Denver, Denver, CO.

[4] Adler, R.B., & Rodman, G. (1998). *Understanding human communication* (6th ed.). New York: Harcourt, Brace College Publishers, 24–25.

[5] Dance, F.E.X., & Zak-Dance, C.C. (1994). *Speaking your mind: Private thinking and public speaking.* Dubuque, IA: Kendall Hunt Publishing, 29.

[6] See Verderber.

[7] Gardner, H. (1983). *Frames of mind: The theory of multiple intelligences.* New York: Basic Book Publishers.

[8] See Verderber.

[9] See Adler, & Rodman, 23.

[10] Carrell, L. J. (1997). "Diversity in the communication curriculum: Impact on student empathy." *Communication Education,* 46(4), 234–244.

[11] See Adler, & Rodman, p. 24, citing research of Hamacheck, (1987). *Encounters with the self* (2nd ed.). Fort Worth, TX: Holt, Rinehart, and Winston, 8.

[12] See Adler, & Rodman, 22–24.

[13] Stott, J. (1973). *Only one way: The message of Galatians.* Downers Grove, IL: InterVarsity Press, 148.

[14] Farris, S. (1998). *Preaching that matters: The Bible and our lives.* Louisville, KY: Westminster Press, 7.

[15] Lutzer, E. (1998). *Pastor to pastor: Tackling the problems of ministry.* Grand Rapids, MI: Kregel Publications, 32.

[16] See Verderber.

[17] Sparks, J.A. (1977). *Pot-shots at the preacher: Handling criti-*

*cism in the church.* Nashville, TN: Abingdon Press, 101.

[18] See Sparks.

[19] See Verdeber, 17.

[20] See Lutzer, 35.

[21] Rowell, E. (1998). *Preaching with spiritual passion: How to stay fresh in your calling.* Minneapolis, MN: Bethany House Publishers, 104.

[22] Olford, S. with Olford, D. (1998). *Anointed expository preaching.* Nashville, TN: Broadman and Holman Publishers.

[23] Howe, R.L. (1967). *Partners in preaching.* New York: The Seabury Press.

[24] Postman, N. (1985). *Amusing ourselves to death.* New York: Viking Penguin.

[25] Hauerwas, S., & Willimon, W.H. (1992). *Preaching to strangers.* Louisville, KY: John Knox Press.

[26] Tisdale, L.T. (1997). *Preaching as local theology and folk art.* Minneapolis, MN: Augsburg Fortress Press.

[27] Dance, F.E.X. (1973). "Speech communication: The revealing echo." In L. Thayer (Ed.), *Communication: Ethical and moral issues* (pp. 277–285). New York: Gordan and Breach.

[28] See Verderber.

[29] See Adler, & Rodman.

[30] See Trenholm.

[31] See Dance, & Zak-Dance, 3.

[32] Anderson, J. (1984). *Outspoken women: Speeches by American women reformers, 1635–1935.* Dubuque, IA: Kendall Hunt Publishers, 198.

# SECTION 2

# TALK
# TO ONE
# ANOTHER

*"My preacher likes to know we have been listening."*
A LISTENER

Chapter 4

# Listeners' Leanings

I N THE FIRST SECTION OF THIS BOOK, we clarified the communication perspective through which we will be examining preaching. Now let's have a look at the results of
*The Great American Sermon Survey.*
Listeners talk about sermons all the time. They talk with spouses,
children, and friends. The sermon suggestions they have to offer
may be perceptive, and yet, those suggestions are offered primarily
in self-talk or to a trusted friend who will keep the info confidential.

Yes, listeners certainly talk about the sermon . . . they just don't
talk *to the preacher* about the sermon. They protect him, they care
about her, they fear him, they don't know him well enough, or
they don't think she has the time. Many have just been taught, by
years of tradition, that in church we are passive, we "sit still and
shut up." Perhaps it's that monologue model of human communication haunting us again. If we have a problem with the sermons,
we can examine our own spiritual lives to see what is lacking; we
can church hop; or we can spend sermon time daydreaming, with
eyes glazed or glaring toward the pulpit.

Some surveyed listeners said,

- "Growing up Catholic, I have never seen a parishioner
  discussing a homily with a priest."
- "There is not a time or place for dialogue of that sort in
  church."

It's systemic? Well then, let's nudge the system toward a little
change. Understanding one another's perspectives is requisite for

improving communication competence. Listeners want the best sermon interaction possible, as do preachers. For the most part, adult listeners choose to come listen to a sermon, though one 24-year-old listener participating in this sermon survey confesses, "I come because my mom makes me." Since preachers don't get out much on Sunday mornings, most regular church attenders have heard hundreds more sermons than their preachers have heard. Preachers are attempting to affect listeners, yet they are frequently protected from knowing many of the meanings their listeners have made from the sermon. They may be shielded by choice, by the organizational system of the church, by the "loving" reluctance of the listeners to directly criticize the preacher, or by a perception of the listeners that their opinions are irrelevant.

Certainly, other types of public speakers also get only nominal response from their listeners: eye contact, head nods, smiles, applause, a few enthused hand-shakers who make their way to the front, the occasional (figurative) tomato, and perhaps an obligatory thank you note from the organizer of the event. Yes, in other contexts, many speakers hope their message will bring personal profit or votes; they do not necessarily have the best interest of the listeners in mind. In the classroom "public speaking" context, listener benefit *is* a goal. Teachers treasure those few students who become invigorated by the subject matter and go on to make careers founded on the content of a course. While university professors and vocational school instructors receive anonymous written feedback after a course is completed, it is the conversation with students *during* the course that best aids clarity and enthusiasm. The post hoc student evaluation comment, "This is the worst teacher in the world; she gave me a 'C' and often wears navy and black together" is hardly helpful. Once summer rolls around, the classroom is cleaned, chairs turned upside down on desks, relationships end.

In the preaching context, a vital difference exists from many other public speeches: the preacher is in an ongoing relationship with the listeners, the preacher and the listeners are part of a community whose primary challenge is to *love one another*. That's why we don't call the listeners "the audience"—they are not supposed to be a quiescent clump of human culture, but rather a community of individuals on journeys of Christian faith. While all human communication has a relational dimension, it is this intensified relational component that both inhibits and necessitates interaction between listeners and preachers about the sermon.

While many preachers report that they do relish the nodding, smiling, affirming responses some listeners provide during the sermon, gauging the actual impact of the message can be quite complex. Few use altar calls these days. Fewer still have trusted, intimate friends as members of their churches. Many preachers lament the "transient" nature of their church population as a "fact" of modern life, but their call to community still enables the possibility of longer and deeper relationships than most other kinds of public speakers and audience members are able to cultivate.

While preachers may already be a little defensive or hesitant as they approach this chapter, some may be skipping over this introductory material to get to the "goodies." Participating listeners are generally gentle; many adding comments like: "My preacher is great, but *other* preachers I've heard need to stop rambling." "Our preacher is terrific, but I have heard bad sermons from other preachers." "Our pastor is quick, sharp, and makes me think—with most other preachers I am dulled to sleep." Though the survey process promises anonymity, several listeners include remarks like, "If this gets back to my preacher, I am not directly referring to her but to preaching in general." In fact, 99 participants chose not to provide demographic information such as gender, age, church type, church location, or church size. Is it possible that they are worried about their preachers knowing what they really think?

Said many, "I love my preacher." Said one, "We love our preacher. He is part of our church family, but he is not very effective. So we have learned to love him anyway. He needs us and that is a lesson we have all learned."

Of course, many listeners, perhaps feeling silenced for who knows how many years, chose to complete a survey because they had something specific on their minds. Since the surveys did not provide categories of answers, listeners were able to write any response that would fit in the area provided. A majority wrote more than a simple, short phrase; some even filled up the back of the survey sheet with lengthy heart-felt explanations. Say more than a few: "My preacher lets us know he does not care about our opinion," and "My response to the message doesn't matter."

Listeners, your responses do matter. In fact, listener response is the reason for the sermon in the first place. Thank you for sharing your perceptions. We all need to hear what you have to say.

## What kind of people are the participating listeners?

For many listeners, this survey was the first time in their lives they had been asked to describe their perceptions of preaching with the awareness that these perceptions would be made known to preachers. No specific churches or listeners are identified; but, since the selection of churches was random, the listeners who respond represent typical listeners. At least, typical listeners who are willing to complete a survey distributed in their randomly selected church.

How did we find the 479 listeners whose responses are summarized on the following pages? Preachers from Protestant and Catholic churches across the country were *randomly* selected to participate in this study. They were asked to complete a survey, participate in a phone interview, and distribute surveys to their listeners. There were 102 preachers who participated in at least one part of the study; their listeners were then given the opportunity to complete a survey and mail it back to the researcher, anonymously. There were 479 listeners who participated in this sermon survey research.

### Listeners' Age Categories
Ages 19–40:  27 percent
Ages 41–59:  37 percent
Ages 60+:  35 percent

- 61 percent of the listeners are female, while 39 percent are male.

- Listeners' ages range from 19 to 88. The average age of listeners is 52. The most frequently cited age was 40.

## Church Size Category

| | |
|---|---|
| Very Small (10–100): | 29 percent (mostly Protestant) |
| Small (101–200): | 15 percent  (mostly Protestant) |
| Medium (201–400): | 23 percent |
| Large (401–900): | 17 percent |
| Mega (901+): | 15 percent  (mostly Catholic) |

- Listeners from very small, small, medium, large, and mega-sized churches participated. Church sizes range from 10 regular attenders to 6000.
- 60 percent of the listener-respondents are Protestant and 40 percent are Catholic.
- Church size and church type are related: 45 percent of Catholic parishes are in the "mega" category while only 2 percent of Protestant churches are that large. Only 14 percent of Catholic parishes have 200 or less attenders while 60 percent of Protestant churches have under 200 attenders. So most Catholic listeners are part of large or mega parishes while most Protestant listeners are attending small or very small churches.[1]

## Listener Location of Churches

| | |
|---|---|
| Urban: | 16 percent |
| Suburban: | 23 percent |
| Small city: | 41 percent |
| Rural: | 20 percent |

- As we know, churches are everywhere in this country: the suburbs, large and small cities, and rural areas. Listener-participants were from all over: Native American reservations, Western ranch country, Southwestern deserts, the coasts, Midwestern farmland and woodlands, Eastern urban sprawl, Northeastern hamlets, and probably, a church location similar to your own.

## Summary of Listeners' Responses

And what did these listeners have to say? Plenty. What follows is a summary of listeners' responses. Quotations from the listeners are also included to further assist our understanding of one another's perspectives.

### Preparation Time

**Q:** How much time do you think it takes the preacher to prepare a sermon?

**A:** 12 hours.

Ten percent of listeners said something like: "All week and more." "It takes a lifetime." "It's an on-going process." "Three years of seminary plus years of experience." The rest of the listeners (who answered with a number) predicted that preachers prepare anywhere from zero minutes (impromptu) to 60 hours. Because of some of the very high answers, the (mathematical) average was 12 hours of preparation. The most common answer was 2 hours. Ten percent of listeners perceive that sermon preparation takes four or five days of each week. Several listeners reply to this question bluntly: "How should I know?"

### Ideal Length of Sermon

**Q:** How long should the sermon last?

**A:** 22 minutes.

Listeners' answers range from 2 minutes to 60 minutes. Several say something like, "As long as it takes." But the average listener wants the sermon to last 22 minutes. There is a statistically significant negative correlation between listeners' desired sermon length and church size category: the larger the church, the shorter listeners want the sermon to be; the smaller the church, the longer listeners want the sermon to be.[2] There is also a statistically significant relationship between desired length and church type: Catholic listeners want their sermons shorter than do Protestants.[3]

Catholic Listeners:      15 minutes

Protestant Listeners:   25 minutes

Listeners also perceive that shorter sermons take less preparation time.[4]

## Nervousness

**Q:** Do you think most preachers feel nervous before preaching?

**A:** Yes.

Fifty-seven percent of listeners believe their preachers are nervous, while the other 43 percent do not.

## Listeners' Inner Reactions

**Q:** What is your inner reaction to most sermons you hear?

**A:** Generally positive.

Thirty-one percent of listeners have a generally negative reaction, though a majority of listeners had some kind of general or specific positive reaction. Those positive reactions have been separated into four types: heightened spirituality, general positive statement, relevance, and increased readiness to change. Even those who have a generally positive reaction had many specific pieces of advice, which they offer to preachers later in the survey.

- 31 percent of listeners have a generally negative inner reaction to most sermons that they hear. They label the sermons: irrelevant to my life, disappointing, little trite talks, repetitive, ho-hum, or not well prepared.

- 20 percent of the listeners describe an inner reaction of heightened spirituality indicating that they are closer to God, inspired, refocused on God, peaceful, and/or more hopeful after hearing a sermon.
- 19 percent of the listeners describe a general (rather than specific) positive reaction such as: "I feel good," "I'm glad I came," "I'm thankful," "It was enjoyable," or "It was a decent sermon."
- 15 percent of listeners indicate that they either find relevance or their inner reaction is an attempt to find relevance. Answers include: "I try to connect it to my life if possible," "It was relevant," "I usually get some insight for daily living," or "I am able to find direct application of Scripture." Says one listener, "My inner reaction to most sermons I hear is, 'What about me?' "
- 14 percent of listeners say that their typical reaction is an increased readiness to change an attitude, belief, action, or value. One listener admits, "Sometimes he kicks me right in the bum." While almost all of this 14 percent speak of *personal* changes, only one listener mentions social change.

### Why Listeners Listen

**Q:** Why do you listen to sermons?

**A:** A desire for inspiration or life application.

- 35 percent of listeners want to be inspired by the sermon.
- 30 percent of the listeners listen for life application ideas.
- 21 percent of the listeners are hoping to gain information or increase understanding.
- 14 percent of the listeners yearn for insight.

Catholics and Protestants listen to sermons for the same reasons, and listeners of various-sized churches listen to sermons for the same reasons. Women and men listen to sermons for the same reasons. But *church location* and *age* make a difference!

While a majority of listeners in every location want either *inspiration* or *life application* from their sermons, urban listeners reverse the top two answers. Urbanites want life application more than inspiration and they have less interest in *insight* than other listeners do. Suburbanites are least interested in listening to gain information.[5] Listeners ages 41–59 are more concerned with *life application* than younger or older listeners. The oldest listeners (60–88) are much more interested in *inspiration* (and much less interested in *insight*) than younger listeners.[6]

Comments from the listeners include:

- "Be uplifting. Life is hard enough—don't keep telling us what sinners we are—we are the believers! Tell us we're human and that's okay. We know we need to strive for better always."
- "Relate the Bible to our lives today."
- "I try to listen more closely when the information relates to my life."
- "I come to church stressed, tired. I need inspiration to lift me up for another week. That's why I come."
- "I enjoy hearing the thoughts of Biblical scholars as they are overlaid on our present-day society. I'm looking for religious relevance to today's questions."

### Talking to the Preacher about the Sermon

**Q:** Do you regularly talk to the preacher about his/her sermons?

**A:** No.

Whether male or female, Catholic or Protestant, young, middle aged, or older—listeners respond to this question with a loud, nearly unison, "No. I do not talk to my preacher about the sermon." What about listeners who say that the sermon has more impact on their lives than any other component of the church service? The answer does not change. Most people who listen to sermons in the United States at the turn of the millennium do not talk to the preacher regularly about the sermon.[7]

The 78 percent that say they do not talk to the preacher about the sermon, were asked, "Why not?" Sixty-four percent say they don't talk to the preacher because of "lack of time." Says one, "He's obviously too busy just to chat with someone." Another 24 percent of the listeners don't talk to the preacher regularly because, "It's not my place to tell the preacher how to do his job" or "I don't want her to think I'm questioning her." Finally, 12 percent of the listeners don't talk to the preacher because either, "The preacher does well, so I don't need to say anything," or "If there's ever anything especially meaningful, I'll let the preacher know."

Comments from the listeners include:

- "We have two pastors—one loves to hear how we react to his homilies and welcomes our remarks—the other pastor doesn't really encourage any communication. If I tell him some point I liked, learned, or needed, he brushes my compliments off as if he doesn't care to hear the compliment. He is so confident, he knows there is nothing I could say that would affect him one way or another."
- "I have tried to talk to the one who loses his place in his notes and mutters; he could really care less."
- "No, I don't talk to the preacher but I think it's important for many people to give our priests feedback. It builds our priests up and in turn they build us up—that's what it is to build up the kingdom of God."
- "It's just not my place."
- "He's doing his job; I'm doing mine. He talks. I listen."

### What Listeners Gained from a Sermon

**Q:** Describe something you gained (or learned) from a specific sermon?

**A:** (A majority could do so.)

Sixty-eight percent of the listeners had an answer, while 32 percent could not remember something gained from a specific sermon. Of those who could describe something they gained from a specific sermon, 26 percent gained clarification on some doctrinal or theological issue, 22 percent remembered a belief or attitude change, 21 percent recalled a Biblical fact, 20 percent mentioned God's love for them, 6 percent explained a point of church or Biblical history, while 5 percent recalled assistance with the process of forgiveness.

Comments from the listeners include:

- "Repent does not mean just being vocally contrite. It means 'Stop what you are doing and change for the better.'"
- "Insight into nature of 'Powers and Principalities' and their influence. Not disembodied spirits, but social institutions."
- "I became a believer."
- "Learned the wise men didn't come immediately after Jesus was born but much later."
- "I've learned that God will never leave me or forsake me. He loves and cares about me, with a love that I can hardly comprehend."
- "That God is real, and He is alive, and he loves me personally . . . He loves me that much and the knowledge of that love has changed my life."
- "I learned how and why to forgive."
- "I got saved."
- "Our pastor gave a sermon on communion coins once. He collects coins as a hobby. I learned the practices of Protestant churches in Scotland and England regarding giving of communion 200–300 years ago—examination, giving of the coin, presentation to be served."
- "Jacob was a grabber who always wanted to be in control. His life had great importance only when God took over and was the motivator. In my life, I don't always have to be in control, even when the situation is one where I have experience and strong ideas. Things don't have to be 'my way or else.' Let go and let God."
- "That one needs to accept one's unique situation and per-

sonality—all one's strengths and weaknesses because that is God's gift. Be who you are—because that's whom God created and loves. Trust that is enough for God and the ones you serve."

- "I learned that I can have all kinds of knowledge about the Christ, but unless I see my need for him and turn my way of living around, it is all useless."

### Good Sermons

**Q:** What makes a sermon good?

**A:** A relevant message; good content.

Fifty percent of the listeners say that a good sermon has relevant content; many also say good sermon content provides insight or provokes thought by relating Bible or God-centered precepts to daily life. Says one listener: "Please concentrate on the children and youth. If they haven't found relevancy in the church by the time they're eighteen, they probably won't be back when the choice to attend becomes their own." Says another, "My preacher excels at taking current events and 'pop culture' and integrating them into the narrative of scriptural analysis."

Twenty-eight percent of the listeners describe a good sermon as a well-organized sermon. To them, a well organized sermon includes detectable, thorough preparation by the preacher ("The preacher brings insight we don't already have," or "You can tell he does his homework"); clarity ("When he's done, we all know the main point we're supposed to take home with us"); and a well-demonstrated link between the Scripture and the key point(s) of the sermon ("I really don't want just good advice or common sense wisdom from the sermon. I can get that from Katie Couric on the Today Show").

The final group of listeners, 21 percent, describe a good sermon as one that is well delivered. Explanations of good delivery include creativity, sincerity, warmth, conversational manner, the ability to hold attention, and vocal passion. "I appreciate any attempts the preacher makes to be creative," says a surveyed listener.

There is no relationship between the descriptions of good sermons and the reasons people listen to sermons. So those who want inspiration and those who want insight still agree on the characteristics of a good sermon:

(1) Meaningful content.
(2) Good organization, clearly delineated connections to Scripture and to God.
(3) Sincere, warm, and passionate delivery, with some attempts at creativity or at least variety.

Protestants and Catholics agree about what makes a good sermon. Those from tiny rural churches and mega urban parishes also concur. But there is one factor that does make a difference. There is a strongly significant relationship between age category and responses to the question "What makes a good sermon?"[8] Those in the middle category (41–59) find good sermons to be more about *relevant messages* than do their seniors in the 60+ category. (Remember, when asked why they listen, seniors were more interested in *inspiration*.) Listeners ages 19–40 are least likely to call a good sermon a *well organized sermon* while listeners 60 and over are more concerned with *organization* than the other age groups. Yet, regardless of age category, listeners have similar descriptions of a well-delivered sermon.

### Bad Sermons

**Q:** What makes a sermon bad?
**A:** Disorganization; useless content; poor delivery.

Forty-seven percent of listeners say a bad sermon is a disorganized sermon. Their primary description of *disorganization* is the word "rambling," heard over and over and over again from the listeners. They describe lengthy sermons which continue (with repetitive explanation or seemingly unrelated tangents) long after the point has been made, or sermons with so many points that a key thought is difficult to detect. Says one listener, "I wonder if even he knows his main idea and could say it in a sentence." As a secondary note, listeners describe disorganized sermons as those without clear connections to Scripture.

Twenty-eight percent of the listeners say that a bad sermon is a sermon with *useless content*. Most of those who talk about poor content mention a lack of insight or an agenda the preacher is pushing (usually on what listeners perceive to be a tangential rather than essential part of Christianity). Many more mention repetitive content while a few talk about their intense aversion to being "shamed" from the pulpit on a regular basis. Some listeners mention their dislike for sermons that display male bias and others dislike the preacher disclosing only positive information about himself or herself.

Fully one quarter, (25 percent) of the listeners, say a bad sermon is a *poorly delivered* sermon. They are consistent about what makes a poor delivery: monotone reading and use of preacher jargon. (Those who answer, "Don't read to me," often write in large, dark letters and include many exclamation points.)

Comments include:

- "It doesn't sound like he cares about the message or the listeners."
- "If you don't care or prepare, why should I?"
- "I can read too, you know."

There is an almost significant relationship between bad sermons and why people listen.[9] While not statistically significant, it is worthy of our consideration. Those who want *insight* are a little less concerned about organization than other listeners are; those who want *life application* and *inspiration* are more concerned with *relevant content* and *delivery* than are those who want *information*.[10] Age category, church type, and church size didn't matter here. There was agreement: A bad sermon is rambling, irrelevant, repetitive, and/or read with very little vocal variation.

## What Most Impacts the Listeners

**Q:** What component of the church service has the most impact on your spiritual life?

**A:** The sermon.

The answers regarding spiritual impact fell as follows:
35 percent:  Sermon
20 percent:  Communion
18 percent:  Prayer
16 percent:  Music
11 percent:  Liturgy, skits, testimony, and "other" components

Though Catholic and Protestant listeners agree that the sermon is the component of the church service that has the most impact on their spiritual lives, there is a highly significant difference between Protestants and Catholics regarding the priority of other parts of the church service.[11]

For Protestant listeners, the order fell as follows: Sermon (36 percent), Prayer (21 percent), Music (18 percent), Communion (17 percent), and Liturgy, etc. (8 percent).

For Catholic listeners: Sermon (31 percent), Music (27 percent), Liturgy, etc. (17 percent), Communion (16 percent), and Prayer (9 percent).

## Listeners' Advice for Preachers

**Q:** If you could get one message across to all preachers in the United States, what would it be?

**A:** (Many and varied; see below.)

- "Make the message relevant and meaningful."
- "Improve your relationships with listeners."

- "Attend to your own spiritual life."
- "Get your sermons organized."
- "Work on your sermon delivery."
- "We appreciate your work."

Thirty-six percent of the listeners advise preachers regarding their content; most of all, they want a relevant message with clear ties to Scripture. They also urge preachers to have God-centered messages, God-directed messages, and challenging messages. They advise the preachers not to "pound"—literally or figuratively. (Some of this 36 percent report feeling pounded from the pulpit to be more politically liberal or conservative.) A few listeners delineate topic suggestions that they perceive as "neglected": evangelization, family life, heaven, and the relationship of "tolerance and love."

Comments include:

- "I keep hearing about pro-life issues; there is no mention of how we can show Christ's compassion in practical ways—for the quality of life—to the already living babies and children who are abused, neglected, or hungry. Then when they grow up into the welfare system, we'll blame them for not being hard workers in this land of opportunity."
- "Don't allow personal gripes or pet peeves to be the main focus of a homily. It's so whiny."
- "We get mostly nice little talks about what we should or shouldn't do; most are superficial and bland."
- "People shouldn't have to be put down to be persuaded to be a Christian or a more mature Christian."
- "We get encouraged to be nice, be kind, have a positive attitude. How is that different from everybody else? What does it have to do with the Bible or God?"
- "We put a lot of stock in what you say. Be sure it's Biblical and God-directed."
- "I am trying to tell my friend about Christ's love. I don't want to bring her to church because she is so down on herself already. She needs hope, forgiveness, and practical suggestions."

- "The de-moralization of America, the lying president, the use of abortion as birth control—all that stuff we hear about so much—we already know and we are not rooting for it. We're on the same side; why do you seem to preach against us? I just don't need to be put down over and over. My problems are about how to love my neighbor, raise my kids, get through bad times."

Seventeen percent of the listeners suggest that preachers foster relationships with listeners. The most common answer in this category is, "Know your listeners." Others say:

- "Preach with us, not at us."
- "Be real."
- "Get along."
- "Don't show favoritism."
- "Get to know us and let us know you."
- "Be a real person in front of your congregation."
- "Don't try to appear perfect and unable to make a mistake or ask 'Why?' sometimes."
- "It's easier to relate to a pastor who is 'more like everyone else' than someone who is very reserved and aloof."
- "Show your human side. We all look up to you but want to know that you also share the same thoughts and feelings as us."
- "Why doesn't he find a story from a church member and use that as a positive example instead of telling us again how great he is? He wouldn't have to name names, but then we might know he notices we're doing something right."
- "Trust the wisdom of the people of God; trust the Spirit's presence within all the people. Male and female, young and old, of all races and economic levels. Allow them to also share their experiences with God."
- "My preacher is wonderful. He is quite real and genuine with me and other church members. He is willing to listen to feedback."
- "Relate to your congregation. Not everyone was born and

raised in the specific community where the building is located."

- "They're men. I think that sums up the whole problem for preachers. At least, that is, if you're a woman."
- "A former pastor shared the heartache of his experience as an abused child and raising a wayward son. [That] took great courage and I, as a parent, took courage from it."
- "Know your congregation—individually and as a group."
- "Our pastor is always helping others. He is 6′4″ but his heart is the biggest part of his body."

Another 17 percent of the listeners had one message for preachers: Work on your own spiritual life. Listeners want preachers to:

- "Preach from your spiritual journey so messages are genuine."
- "Be a model of a deeply spiritual person."
- "Pray more."
- "Recognize the power of your words."
- "Give 100 percent of your effort."
- "Don't neglect your family."
- "Check your motives."
- "I've had an angry preacher and a preacher who was unethical. In contrast, I've had two preachers I feel were closely connected to God. That closeness was reflected in their sermons and daily actions. Preachers, you need a close relationship with God to be effective."
- "Work on your own spiritual life. It shows."

There were 15 percent of the listeners who want preachers to improve sermon organization. As before, the complaints involve rambling and the often missing link between Scripture and key points. Say listeners:

- "Preachers, know your main point so we can too."
- "Do your research."
- "Use a variety of organizational strategies."
- "Make the message clear, simple, interesting, with one suggested action and one benefit."

- "If I have to hear about [a particular topic] one more time, I'm going to walk out of this church and never look back. It's not that I don't want to be confronted with sin, but we're pretty much all believers here."
- "Don't harp on a subject over and over. Make your point and go on. Many people have told me that this is one thing that turns them off of a sermon or pastor. For example, [from the pulpit] openly telling people to greet visitors even though the people do it. Or comments about the deacons when everybody knows who they are."
- "Usually there is too much to digest at one sitting."
- "Save those other points for another sermon."
- "Doesn't the preacher want to get to the dinner table just like some of his flock?"
- "Sometimes they start off well and then get lost or off target. Many miss the mark and I wonder what the speaker is trying to say. I wonder how much they prepared."

Then there were 9 percent of listeners who want preachers to hear this message: Work on your delivery. They advise preachers against using jargon, reading, and passionless vocal expression. Some also say:

- "Show your sense of humor."
- "Don't try so hard to be funny that you get too 'cutesy.'"
- "Why doesn't he know how regular people talk? He's just trying to show us how much smarter and more spiritual he is."
- "Talk on a level everyone can understand."
- "Don't talk down to your congregation, but also don't talk way over our heads."
- "I can read too. If you're just going to mumble through a manuscript, make copies to hand out and skip the sermon."
- "Do not put a piece of paper between you and me—five minutes spoken from the heart by a person trained in the field can do more for me than any written sermon. I can read from any book of sermons when I am studying."
- "What a waste of time to read the Scripture twice in a row.

The second reading just fills up time so he has even less homily to prepare."

Finally, 5 percent of listeners identified their one message as: "You are appreciated," saying:

- "Thank you."
- "Don't ever quit."
- "You make a difference."

From the 479 listeners, there were 58 different responses to the question: "If you could get one message across to all preachers in the United States, what would it be?" Five of the responses didn't fit a category, including: "Get a better sound system; I can't hear you so it doesn't matter what you say," and "Don't have people touch my communion food—gross!" There was also a piece of advice for the researcher: "Get a real job."

Based on the mathematical averages as well as the most common and majority responses, we can create a "typical listener" profile. Obviously, there are many different styles of listeners. The following represents a compilation of characteristics which are representative of themes emerging from the responses.

## Typical Listener Profile

The typical listener is a 52-year-old woman. Let's call her Linda. If she is a Protestant, she attends a church of 400 or less in the suburbs or a small city; if she is a Catholic, she attends a parish with at least 400 other listeners, though it is probably even larger than 900 attenders.

Linda predicts that her preacher can prepare a sermon in twelve hours or less and hopes he will preach for twenty-two minutes or less. If she is Catholic and/or attends a large church (over 900), she wants her homily to last about fifteen minutes. She perceives that the longer the sermon, the more her preacher has prepared.

Linda thinks her preacher is nervous. Her common response to most sermons is a "generally negative" reaction such as "ho-hum." If she doesn't have a negative reaction, she reports feeling "closer to God" after the sermon. Linda does not perceive the sermon as relevant to her daily life nor does it prompt her to make any changes. She listens hoping for inspiration or life application. (If she is in an urban or suburban location, she especially does not want to hear an "informative" sermon. Her desire for life application is highest right now, while she is between 40 and 59 years old.)

She does not talk to her preacher about the sermon because there is no time or mechanism for dialogue. Linda can describe something she gained from a specific sermon; it will likely be related to a specific circumstance in her life. For her, a good sermon has a relevant, meaningful message and a bad sermon "rambles." If her preacher reads a manuscript, she is adamantly negative about such a delivery process. She wants a "passionate" delivery, key points which are clearly linked to Scripture, and most of all, relevancy.

When compared to other components of the church service, the sermon has the "most impact" on Linda's spiritual life. Even with that acknowledgment, Linda still has advice to offer. If she could get one message across to preachers in the U.S. she would say one of the following:

- *Provide a relevant message with clear ties to Scripture* (for example, she dislikes even relevant advice from the preacher without Biblical depth or insight—she can get that from Oprah or many other sources);
- *Foster relationships with your listeners* (so you can be relevant; so you can demonstrate God's love, so you can preach with, not at);
- *Work on your own spiritual life* so sermons can be insightful, deep, and sincere. (Linda believes she can judge the depth of the preacher's spiritual life during the sermon; for example, if he reads in a monotone, he's not passionate about God or his topic; if the preacher presents shallow "nice little talks," she perceives his spiritual life is not deep or that he is condescending; if he continually states obvious platitudes, she again thinks his spiritual life is not deep).

## Summary

To complete our examination of listeners' leanings expressed in *The Great American Sermon Survey*, let's spend just a few more minutes "listening" to the following representative quotations from listeners' surveys.

- "Genuine enthusiasm displayed by the preacher on behalf of the message of Jesus will do more to enrich the spiritual lives of the congregation than any other element contained within the sermon."
- "A good sermon, like a good speech, needs to have an opening, a body, and a closing. You must know your congregation—try to relate to each age group, young and old. A sense of humor is always nice. A good sermon is delivered with love. A bad sermon is where the message is delivered with no emotion or feeling—one must not be condescending. A bad sermon does not acknowledge or relate to the present day issues and Biblical teaching."
- "An effective sermon is well prepared, completely grounded in Scripture, and delivered with genuine enthusiasm. An ineffective sermon can be one that is too academic for a general audience. Hasty preparation, shaky logic, and mumbling in a monotone are all additional ingredients in ineffective sermons."
- "Needs to be well thought through, relevant to current situation, expressed in language easily understood. Sermons that are too erudite, too lofty, too adamant, or closed-minded turn me off. On controversial issues, I want to know both sides, but be persuaded to one."
- "Get to the point. Try to speak in everyday language and try to relate the gospel story to day to day living."
- "Know the techniques of effective public speaking."
- "Offer spiritual meat for us to use during the week—not just 'feel good' or superficial platitudes. Be more insightful and less ordinary."

- "Look at the congregation and talk with them, don't read to them. Don't talk down to the congregation as if they are beneath you. Help lead the congregation to excellence in their Christian journey."

## Notes

[1] There was a highly significant chi-square for listener church type and listener church size: $p \leq .000001$.

[2] $r = -.318$; $p \leq .0001$

[3] t-test F=17.494; $p \leq .0001$

[4] $r=.1347$; $p = .006$

[5] $p = .032$

[6] $p = .019$

[7] * No statistically significant relationship between listener gender and whether or not a listener talks to preacher about sermon ($p = .671$); no statistically significant relationship between church type and whether or not a listener talks to preacher about sermon ($p = .781$); no statistically significant relationship between component of church service with most impact and whether or not a listener talks to preacher about sermon ($p = .229$); and no statistically significant relationship between age category and whether or not a listener talks to preacher about sermon ($p = .332$).

[8] $p=.015$

[9] $p=.067$

[10] $p=.061$

[11] $p \leq .001$

# Chapter 5

# Preachers' Perspectives

KAY, PREACHERS. We listen to you for 22 minutes or so, once a week, but it's just not enough. We want to hear more. We need to understand your perspective of preaching. What are your goals? What are your challenges? What do you think of us sitting out here looking up toward you?

As you read this chapter, remember, the preachers sharing their perspectives here are the communication partners of the listeners whose responses you just finished reading in Chapter Four. The preacher-participants in this study were selected from lists of U.S. Protestant churches and Catholic parishes. A random sampling procedure was used to select potential participants. This type of selection process provides participants from across the country who represent what is "typical" by giving us access to a wide variety of churches. Letters of explanation were mailed, inviting the randomly selected preachers to participate. Those 102 preachers who chose to complete sermon surveys, provide interviews, and/or distribute listener surveys became the preacher-participants for *The Great American Sermon Survey*.

Scheduling the telephone interviews proved to be quite a challenge; preachers are busy people who absolutely must use pencil or erasable ink in their daily planners. Their schedules seem to be interrupted several times a day. Many preachers were called away at the last minute for illnesses and deaths in their church community. One preacher missed an interview time, then called back later, leaving this message, "I'm sorry I wasn't here when you called. I meant to be, but I was in jail. I mean, I was down at the jail. Not for me, you know, for one of my . . ." The short-tempered answering machine cut him off. Another preacher came up from the church basement to get the phone, asking if we could talk in thirty minutes—after he'd had a shower. Apparently, he was fulfilling the role of emergency plumber, cleaning out a clogged sewer pipe at the time we'd scheduled our interview. For those who were able to talk about preaching, thank you. The conversations were engaging and memorable. Those who give their lives in service to others have fascinating stories to tell . . .

. . . to the preacher laboring in a tiny Southern church of ten faithful attenders,

. . . to the preacher of a Midwestern mega church whose deep understanding of preaching could fill the pages of several volumes,

. . . to the humble Western preacher who didn't recognize his own strengths of love and warmth, communicated even in his voice as he spoke through the telephone line,

. . . to the singing priest whose insights are routinely profound,

. . . to the dynamic Jewish Christian preacher who organizes his church community to actively love one another in the most practical of ways,

. . . to the preacher from the great Northwest who listens intently to his listeners,

. . . and to the many more women and men whose job it is to preach our sermons . . .

*Thank you* for giving your time and thoughts so listeners can better understand your perspective. Thank you, preachers, for sharing your hearts and minds.

Two kinds of responses are summarized in this chapter. From the interviews, a qualitative analysis of data was used to derive *themes* upon which a majority of preachers agree. Representative preacher quotes are used to illustrate the themes. From the surveys, quantitative data have been derived to help us understand percentages, averages, and relationships of different kinds of answers.

## What kind of people are the participating preachers?

- 84 percent of the preachers are male, while 16 percent are female.
- Preachers' ages range from 24–82. The average age of preachers is 51.
- 83 percent of the preachers are Protestant, while 17 percent are Catholic.
- Preachers report their church sizes as ranging from 10–6000.

### Church Size Category

| | |
|---|---|
| Very Small (10–100): | 20 percent |
| Small (101–200): | 27 percent |
| Medium (201–400): | 21 percent |
| Large (401–900): | 16 percent |
| Mega (901+): | 16 percent |

Remember from Chapter Four that there is a statistically significant association between church type and church size category. The mega-size churches are mostly Catholic, while the small and very small churches are mostly Protestant.

### Preacher Location of Churches

| | |
|---|---|
| Urban: | 12 percent |
| Suburban: | 23 percent |
| Small city: | 41 percent |
| Rural: | 23 percent |

## Summary of Preachers' Responses

Let's begin by trying to ascertain how typical preachers prepare for their sermons.

### Preparation Time

**Q:** What is the average (typical) amount of time you spend preparing a sermon?

**A:** 9 hours.

Preachers prepare for each sermon from 2–41 hours. The (mathematical) average for preparation time is 9 hours, though the most frequently mentioned, hourly figure is 8. Only 4 percent take four or five full workdays for sermon preparation. Many describe an "incubation" process, which may take days. In this "incubation" stage, preachers (after reading and studying the text) turn on a "heightened awareness" as they look for insight related to the sermon topic from their experiences during the week.

Very few preachers prepare the sermon all in one day, but rather do a little sermon prep here and there throughout the week. A majority of preachers finish sermon preparation on Friday or Saturday, while a few don't feel "ready" until they step into the pulpit.

Three preachers describe a preparation process that has them planning topics months in advance, while most who use a lectionary for topic and text selection work primarily week by week.

Though some preachers lament failing memories as they age, there is not a statistically significant relationship between preparation hours and the preacher's age.

There is a statistically significant relationship between church type and preparation time.[1] The average preparation time for a Catholic priest is 3 hours; for a Protestant preacher, it is 11 hours.

### Preacher Preparation Processes

**Q:** List the kinds of activities that are a part of your sermon preparation process.

**A:** Studying the Biblical text.

Following is a list of the type of preparation process and the percentage of preachers who use that process in their sermon preparation.

| | |
|---|---|
| Studying the Biblical text: | 73 percent |
| Gathering supportive evidence: | 53 percent |
| Consulting commentaries: | 52 percent |
| Drafting/writing manuscript or outline: | 48 percent |
| Prayer: | 41 percent |
| Incubating/reflecting/pondering: | 35 percent |
| Topic selection: | 13 percent |
| Revision: | 15 percent |
| Oral rehearsal: | 12 percent |
| Consulting listeners: | 9 percent |

Forty-nine percent of preachers also list one idiosyncratic preparation strategy like talking to their spouses, working at the soup kitchen, or jogging.

As you think about these answers, remember, preachers did not select their responses from a list, they just wrote down what they do while preparing their sermons. So, we don't know whether or not some pray about the sermon but don't think of it as officially part of what they do on Tuesday mornings during their three hours of blocked out "sermon preparation time." Perhaps some preachers will read this list and think, "Oh, incubation. I do that. I just never thought of it that way." Since most preachers report using a manuscript or outline, we know they must spend time composing it though only 48 percent list that writing as a component of their preparation. So the results are difficult to interpret but we can discern some obvious trends.

- Most preachers spend sermon preparation time studying the Biblical text, gathering supportive evidence, and consulting commentaries.

- Most preachers do not spend preparation time consulting listeners or rehearsing orally. Of the 9 percent who do consult listeners as they prepare for the sermon, almost all do so informally. In fact, only *one* (of the 102 preachers) describes a currently used, formal procedure for involving listeners in sermon preparation.

Those who use each of the preparation strategies listed above, also rank ordered the strategies in terms of time and effort:

(1)   Studying the Biblical text
(2)   Consulting listeners
(3)   Incubating
(4)   Praying
(5)   Consulting commentaries
(6)   Writing outline/manuscript
(7)   Gathering supportive evidence
(8)   Selecting topic
(9)   Rehearsing orally
(10)  Revising

- Most preachers use most of their preparation time and effort to study the Biblical text.
- Very few preachers (9 percent) mention consulting listeners as part of their preparation process, but those who do, say it takes more time and effort than all other kinds of preparation tasks except text study. And remember, all but one of those 9 percent are consulting listeners in an irregular and informal way.
- Though less than half of the preachers pray as they are preparing their sermons, those who do pray (41 percent) see prayer as taking less time and energy than text study.
- Though very few preachers (12 percent) rehearse orally, those who do say it doesn't take much time and effort compared to the other preparation tasks. From the interviews we know that some preachers rehearsed sermons orally in the beginning of their preaching ministry, but no longer find it "necessary" or "possible."

Says one dedicated oral rehearser who also shares his sense of humor: "We have to rehearse so we can say we 'practice what we preach.' "

Reports another: "Oral rehearsal makes me more conversational and allows me to have better, real eye contact. I work to avoid the 'preacher voice' my wife notices . . . I get out from behind the pulpit—just like the change from Cronkite to Brokaw—the more they see of you, the more they can sense your sincerity and truthfulness."

## Preacher Supporting Material

**Q:** Besides Biblical information, what kinds of supporting material do you most typically use as illustration in your sermon?

**A:** Stories.

The supporting material for illustrations fell as follows:

| | |
|---|---|
| Narrative (stories, personal anecdotes): | 39 percent |
| Real life (history/current events): | 30 percent |
| Creative efforts (visual aids, drama, video clip, jokes, etc.): | 24 percent |
| Media references (movies, television shows, magazine articles, etc.): | 7 percent |

In the interviews, preachers reveal that almost all of them are aware that narrative is powerful though almost none of them have had direct instruction in the oral art of storytelling. Many are continually looking for "good stories" from preaching magazines, preaching sites on the Internet, current events, historical events, and (a few) even consult their listeners for stories. Preachers' perceptions of "story" or "narrative" in sermons range from using brief self-disclosive anecdotes to illustrate a main point to portraying Biblical characters by "telling" their story in first-person voice.

## Ideal Length of Sermon

**Q:** What is the ideal sermon length?

**A:** 20 minutes.

Preachers' answers range from 5–45 minutes. The average answer is 20 minutes, while the most common answer is 15 minutes. Several preachers did note that the ideal time they list and their actual time are not the same; yes, the sermon frequently takes longer than they plan.

There is a statistically significant relationship between church type and ideal length of sermon. For Catholic priests, the ideal sermon length is 9 minutes; for the Protestant preachers, it is 22 minutes.

**Q:** Preachers, why is that length ideal?

**A:** The attention span of our listeners.

- 66 percent justify their ideal length as being appropriate for the attention span of listeners.
- 20 percent explain, "That's the amount of time I need to develop my sermon topics."
- 7 percent answer, "That's the length my church tradition expects."
- 6 percent give assorted other reasons for the ideal sermon length.

Older preachers do not identify a longer "ideal length" than younger preachers do; there is no statistically significant difference between the "ideal length of a sermon" and a "preacher's age."[2] The longer the sermon, the more preparation time preachers use. There is a statistically significant positive correlation between the preacher's report of preparation hours and the preacher's ideal sermon length.[3]

The pastor of a large, suburban church explains, "Some churchgoers have been trained to expect an hour-long sermon . . . my people would be tired." Other comments include:

- "People have too much to do; I know they're thinking, 'If you are going to use my time, use it valuably.' "
- "Because of TV and commercial structure, people aren't accustomed to sitting more than 12½ minutes."

- "The mind can only comprehend what the rear can endure." (This answer was repeated in many surveys, with four other variations of the word "rear.")

## Nervousness

**Q:** Do you experience nervousness or mental blocks during preparation or preaching?

**A:** No.

Fifty-five percent of preachers report that they are not nervous; 45 percent admit that they do experience nervousness or mental blocks during preparation or preaching. Of those who say "yes," 96 percent mention nervousness, not mental blocks.

**Q:** If you are nervous, why are you nervous?

**A:** The great responsibility of preaching makes me nervous.

Of those who are nervous, 73 percent explain that it is the responsibility of bringing "God's Word," of being "God's Messenger," that makes them nervous. Twenty percent are afraid they'll forget something during the sermon or that "it just won't come together" as they move it from mind through mouth. Seven percent say they have general communication apprehension for any kind of public speaking.

More than half of preachers report that they are not nervous. Such a finding is different than findings in the general population where self-reports of public speaking anxiety are pervasive.

## The Preacher's General Goal

**Q:** What is your general goal (or primary purpose) when you preach?

**A:** To bring about change in the listener.

Among those preachers who identify their style as "teacher," 63 percent have "change" as their general goal, while only 17 percent of those with the "teacher" style want to "transmit information." The answers fell as follows:

Change (attitude, belief, value, or action): 54 percent
Translate (truth of Biblical time/text
    to today's culture): 17 percent
Inspire: 13 percent
Transmit information: 11 percent
Don't know: 4 percent

There is no significant difference between the sermon goals of Protestant and Catholic preachers.

### Predicting Why Your Listeners Listen

**Q:** Why do people come to hear you preach?
**A:** My message is relevant to their lives.

The answers to why preachers believe listeners listen are:

Relevancy of my message: 31 percent
Purpose of my message matches
    their listening goal: 28 percent
Delivery: 18 percent
I don't know (Including, "Ask them, not me"): 17 percent
Succinct (short with a discernible key thought): 5 percent

These answers do not vary for Catholic or Protestant preachers, church size, or preacher gender.

## The Preacher's Greatest Challenge

**Q:** Describe your biggest challenge related to preaching.

**A:** My biggest challenges are related to the content of the sermon.

Message/Content:   37 percent
- "How can I get fresh ideas for familiar content?"
- "To me, the biggest challenge of preaching today is that there is nothing new under the sun. I don't go to the pulpit expecting to tell my people anything new. I don't expect them to say, 'I've never heard that before' but rather, 'I've heard that before, but never that way.' "
- "The relevancy is not always apparent in the text. How can I translate the meaning of some Biblical passages to today's culture?"
- "How can I present difficult but necessary topics well?" The two most frequently mentioned challenging topics are: "Need for money" and "Homosexuality."

Delivery:   35 percent
- "I want to leave my notes behind but it is just too difficult."
- "How can I be creative?"
- "Our delivery itself must communicate love."

Organization:   28 percent
- "I need more preparation time."
- "Organizing my material so that it connects to all the different types of people who are listening is challenging: believers, nonbelievers, young, old, middle-aged, long-time churchgoers, new attenders, etc."

These answers regarding the "greatest challenge" do not differ for Protestant and Catholic preachers.

### Preacher Education

**Q:** Did your education include a course on sermon preparation and delivery?

**A:** 95 percent say: Yes.

**Q:** Of those who say yes, did that course prepare you for the realities of sermon preparation and delivery?

**A:** 68 percent say yes; 32 percent say no.

A third of responding preachers say their education was not adequate for sermon preparation and delivery. Many interviewed preachers describe how dramatically their preaching has changed over the years as they began to understand the people to whom they were preaching.

### Preacher Topic Selection

**Q:** How did you select your last two sermon topics?

**A:** From the lectionary.

The lectionary includes Scripture passages assigned for each week, pre-selected by a governing body of the church. Other preachers prefer selecting a needs-based topic, then finding Scripture related to the topic, such as "Divorce." Some use the seasonal or church calendar, speaking on Lent, for example. Some speak through a series of topics, such as "The Importance of Communion" during a particular month; others through an exegetical series—selecting a text from which to preach over a period of time, for example, "The Book of Luke." Finally, some generally combine pieces of the above, or rely on the Holy Spirit's guidance.

| | |
|---|---|
| Lectionary: | 38 percent |
| Topic/Needs Based: | 20 percent |
| Seasonal/Church Calendar: | 19 percent |
| Series topical: | 8 percent |
| Series exegetical: | 7 percent |
| Other: | 7 percent |

## Preacher Style

**Q:** Choose a word or short phrase that best describes your style of preaching.

**A:** Teacher.

| | |
|---|---|
| Teacher: | 32 percent |
| Connector (Translator): | 25 percent |
| Thought Provoker: | 19 percent |
| Storyteller: | 12 percent |
| Evangelist: | 11 percent |

There is no statistically significant difference between Catholic and Protestant preaching styles. No matter what the preacher's style, "change" is still the number one goal, but there is a significant difference between other types of goals and preaching styles.[4] For example, 63 percent of "teachers" want to change listeners; 17 percent want to transmit information. Sixty percent of "evangelists" want to change listeners; no evangelist has a goal of "transmitting information." Thirty-three percent of "storytellers" want to change listeners, while another 33 percent have as their goal "to inspire." Forty-two percent of "thought provokers" want to change listeners while another 32 percent want to translate from Bible times to today's culture, making the connector style and the thought provoker style more closely related than the other styles.

Interviewed preachers reveal that they feel strongly about their chosen style of preaching, their goal, and their delivery type, as being "the best" or "the right one for me." Says one preacher, "My style matches my temperament and my people." But they disagree about the explicitness of application that is necessary in a sermon. The "thought provokers" are more likely to want listeners to discover application on their own rather than having the sermon include specific directives. It is rare for preachers to consistently incorporate creative methodologies into their sermons. (For example, dressing up as a Biblical character and telling a story in first person; singing popular songs which illustrate the theme from a Scripture reading; performing poetry; using visual aids; etc.). Those who do routinely use such creative methodologies do *not* want to align themselves with the word "performer" as a preaching style. The word has negative connotations of "insincerity" for them.

## Preacher Delivery Style

**Q:** What type of delivery style do you most typically use? (Answer categories were provided for this question, with a write-in "other" category.)

**A:** Extemporaneous (speaking conversationally from a phrase outline).

| | |
|---|---|
| Extemporaneous: | 50 percent |
| Combination of Manuscript and Extemporaneous: | 25 percent |
| Manuscript (Writing the sermon word for word and reading): | 13 percent |
| Memorized (Delivering manuscript from memory): | 8 percent |
| Impromptu (No formal preparation except topic; no notes): | 4 percent |

There is a statistically significant relationship between church type and delivery style.[5] Catholic preachers are much more likely than Protestant preachers to deliver their sermons impromptu. Of those surveyed preachers who deliver sermons impromptu, only 25 percent are Protestant, while 75 percent are Catholic.

## The Preacher's Most Important Task

**Q:** Rank order your ministerial tasks in order of importance.

**A:** Sermon preparation is my most important task.

| | |
|---|---|
| Sermon Preparation (and worship preparation): | 43 percent |
| Pastoral Care (visiting the sick, counseling, etc.): | 25 percent |
| Personal Spiritual Life (prayer, personal Bible reading, etc.): | 18 percent |
| Church Duties (meetings, classes, administration, etc.): | 14 percent |

**Q:** Do preachers spend the most hours on the task they identify as most important?

**A:** 54 percent said no; 46 percent said yes.

There is no significant association between the preacher's most important task and the preacher's general goals, style, or greatest challenge. There is a difference between church type and most important ministerial task, though the difference is not quite statistically significant.[6]

| Most Important Task | Protestant | Catholic |
|---|---|---|
| Sermon prep: | 47 percent | 17 percent |
| Pastoral care: | 23 percent | 17 percent |
| Church duties: | 12 percent | 33 percent |
| Personal spiritual life: | 18 percent | 33 percent |

There may be some role difference between Catholic priests and Protestant ministers: Catholic preachers see their most important tasks as "church duties" and their "personal spiritual lives" (equally) whereas most Protestant preachers identify "sermon preparation" as most important with "pastoral care" as their relatively distant second most important duty. The size of the average Catholic parish is no doubt a factor in the reported role differences.

Over half of both Catholic and Protestant preachers say that they do not spend the most time on the task they rank as most important. So for Protestants, sermon prep is most important, but they don't spend most of their work time on it; and for Catholics, church duties and personal spiritual life are most important, but they don't spend the most time on those activities. (Of course, we would be quick to point out the necessity of teeth brushing and showers, but spend more time on other things. Time spent does not always equal importance, but it's still worthy of our consideration.)

## The Preacher's Role Model

**Q:** If you have a role model for your preaching style, please describe that role model.

**A:** I don't have a role model.

| | |
|---|---|
| No role model: | 51 percent |
| Famous preacher: | 25 percent |
| Personally known preacher: | 18 percent |
| Jesus: | 5 percent |

Since so many Christians are asking "WWJD?" ("What would Jesus do?"), the result on the role model question may surprise some readers. In the interviews, preachers were asked to explain their perceptions of Jesus' preaching. Says one preacher, "Jesus as a role model for preaching? You can't mess with perfection!"

Themes that emerge from those interviews include the following:

- Jesus was a *communicator*. He met people where they were.
- Jesus was a master of *relevancy*; he understood the cultural

history and daily lives of his listeners because he was one of them. He used everyday images to communicate his message.

■ Jesus confronted most "sinners" with *conversation and compassion*; he publicly—even angrily—confronted a specific type of sinner, the hypocrites in the synagogue.

Says a preacher: "Some people have a nineties-style version of Jesus—love, peace, everyone goes home happy. But Jesus confronted sinners, especially hypocrites—calling them a wicked and adulterous generation. He cleared the temple. Sometimes we have to be more confrontive of sin. Jesus ate with sinners, but he didn't participate in their sin. He forgave, but he said, 'Go and sin no more.'"

Another said, "I don't feel the need to confront sin from the pulpit; such conversations are better held privately." Another: "Most people know they are sinners. They don't need me to tell them."

Almost one-third of interviewed preachers concluded that Jesus' style of preaching is not possible or practical in today's church context: Jesus was more dialogic than the "one to many" sermon format we currently use. In addition, Jesus' credibility cannot be rivaled: "He was perfect. There is no perfect church. At least, it wouldn't be after I got there."

And finally, Jesus was here to perform a specific plan of action that does not parallel the goals of today's preachers: "I am not Jesus. I have a different ministry—though I do want to have the mind of Jesus."

### What Preachers Want Their Listeners to Know

**Q:** What would you most like listeners to understand about preaching?

**A:** The time it takes to prepare a worthwhile sermon.

Answers ordered by frequency:

(1)  Listeners need to know the time is takes to prepare a worth-while sermon. "It's not as easy as it looks."

(2)  Listeners need to know that the message of the sermon is from God. "Preaching is God's word to be delivered, not just personal agenda items. If the parking lot needs paving, I don't come up with six reasons why parking lots need to be paved. In a sense, I'm a waiter. My job is to get the food from the kitchen to the table without messing it up."

(3)  "We wish the listeners had more basic Bible knowledge."

(4)  Listeners need to know that they can trust us. "I wish my congregation and all people who sit in churches understood that what they are hearing is coming—in most cases—from individuals who care deeply about their listeners."

(5)  Listeners need to think for themselves. "We provide guidance but relying on us for their entire spiritual understanding is not appropriate."

(6)  Listeners need to know that every sermon cannot be a masterpiece. "The preacher will not be able to deliver a glorious resurrection sermon every Sunday. That's got to be okay. The average church member needs to know the local pastor cannot keep up with Hollywood or Billy Graham. At times he will bomb out. Let them know you love them."

(7)  "Listeners need to know that most preachers would preach themselves to death if someone encouraged them."

## Gathering Listener Responses

**Q:**  How do you know how your listeners are responding to a sermon?

**A:**  Answer Themes:

- *The preacher's primary feedback during the sermon is nonverbal.* "I use a lot of eye contact and I watch their reactions . . . am I beginning to connect? I look for nodding of heads, a raised eyebrow, even a slink back into the chair as if to say, 'Uh-oh. She's talking to me.'"
- *Preachers with a small group of listeners find it easier to give meaning to listeners' nonverbal feedback since they can know each person individually.* "In my previous congregation of 65, I knew each person and could tell by their facial expressions if my sermon was evoking a response."
- *Most preachers do not alter their sermon as they are delivering it, no matter what kinds of listener responses occur.* "One time I did. I was preaching to 350 young people in Canada about how we can be distracted from righteousness. Just then, a fire truck went by with a loud siren. I waited quietly, then said, 'That's exactly what I'm trying to tell you . . . distraction.'" Another, however, said, "I don't pay much attention. If there is a storm on a tin roof, I just speak louder."
- *The typical after-sermon comment is "good sermon" and is given with a handshake at the door or during coffee hour.* It is unusual for preachers to hear specific comments about sermon content; the organizational culture of the church does not seem to create a climate in which such comments occur regularly. "The feedback at the door is much more kind than helpful." One preacher told the story of his first Sunday at a new church when a gentleman greeted him at the door with this comment: "Preacher, in this town, all the church bells go off at noon and I want to make sure you know—that's the time to stop preaching." What a welcome!
- *It is extremely rare for a preacher to have a formal process for soliciting input or instigating dialogue before, during, or after the sermon.* Only one preacher of all interviewed is currently using such a process. Most others

concurred, "I haven't done this probably for the reason that I find people say what they think you want them to say. They might think 'he's insecure' or 'he's fishing for compliments.' They've been trained over the years to say what they think they should."

- *A trusted friend who attends a preacher's church is a rare but great asset.* "There is a tendency in this denomination to be 'friends' with the preacher but not too friendly. To put him on a pedestal. I don't feel superior, but people say they just don't want to bother me. If I need someone to tell my troubles to, I talk to close, long-time friends from out of state, not anyone in my congregation."

- *The longer preachers are in a specific church, the more they are able to see the long-term feedback of changed lives.* "The ultimate way I know people have responded is that they implement the message; they institute a change in behavior."

- *It is extremely rare for preachers to use a dialogic methodology for their sermons;* most would "rarely or never" ask a question for which they wanted a verbal answer from a listener. Of those traditions that do encourage or expect verbal participation during the sermon by the listener, such comments are overwhelmingly positive.

- *Most preachers perceive that they are preaching to people who already believe the basic gospel message.* Though 11 percent "evangelize" during the sermon, most approach the sermon aware that they are preaching primarily to believers. "We are a community of people who believe in Jesus."

- *Many preachers are able to recall listeners whose nonverbal feedback was a great encouragement to them during the sermon, often raising their level of vocal dynamism.* "Old Mrs. Jones—her face was always alive. When there were so many blank stares on the right, I'd zoom back over to look at her face on the left in the front to get the strength to keep going."

## Difficult Listeners

**Q:** Can you describe listeners who are particularly difficult?

**A:** Answer Themes:

- *Difficult listeners communicate that they are not processing the sermon by snoozing, clock watching, avoiding eye contact, and sustaining "blank stares."* Such displays of "indifference" can serve to decrease the preacher's expectancy for what the sermon may accomplish. "One fellow gave me a great compliment: 'I usually have trouble staying awake, but not today.' " Another had a sense of humor about it, "I always joke with them to go ahead and sleep because it'll go directly to their subconscious that way." One pastor noted that, "One of my most difficult listeners gave a real compliment last week: 'Preacher, you didn't blow it today.' " Recalls a long-time preacher, "One listener seated down front fell asleep, her head slipping down onto my wife's shoulder. When it seemed like it couldn't get any worse, she began to snore, loudly."

- *Difficult listeners aren't open to change.* "Many difficult listeners are bitter from life's wounds." "My difficult listener is there every week so that he can say he's been there." "There is something good about being in church. Be there. Be on time. But anything that interferes with the ritual that's been going on for the last 40 years is bad." "Preacher asks questions and waits for an answer—that's disturbing." "The person's rear end is where it ought to be, but the rest of him is in another place or time."

- *Difficult listeners give comments only when they disagree.* "If there's a message for me to call Mr. X, I know I'm in trouble."

- *Difficult listeners have a reactionary mindset; they listen to discover anything that could be judged or perceived negatively.* "They are all watching me to see if I'm going to step in the mud." "The scariest people are those who use righteousness as their weapon." "They are not listening for what I'm saying, but for what they want to hear."

- *Difficult listeners have low expectancy; they do not come ready to listen and may believe they "know it all" already.* They may have developed this low expectancy based on previous sermons that disappointed higher expectations. "For many who think they know all they need to know, the knowing is cerebral, not experiential, not action in their lives."

- *Difficult listeners have often been wounded by another preacher; their defenses are up during the sermon.* Many are angry or hurt. "A church congregation can develop a personality of low expectation." "I came in after another preacher had been asked to leave. The listeners were on the defensive; they were used to being personally named and attacked from the pulpit. It took eighteen months before things started to warm up . . . then one woman said, 'I've finally figured out you're not going to hurt me.'"

Based on the surveys and interviews of preachers, the following "typical preacher profile" has been compiled.

## Typical Preacher Profile

The typical preacher in this study is a 51-year-old male. Let's call him Larry. If he is Protestant, he's preaching in a small city church with 400 or fewer attenders; if he is Catholic, he's preaching in a small or large city church with more than 400 parishioners.

Larry spends eight to nine hours preparing his sermon each week. Most of his preparation time and effort is spent studying the Biblical text for the sermon. He also spends time consulting commentaries and looking for stories to illustrate his message. During this preparation process, he does not usually consult his listeners, rehearse orally, or pray. Larry perceives the ideal sermon length to be twenty minutes because he believes that is the length of his listeners' attention span, though, if he is Catholic he knows his listeners want his homily to be even shorter so he aims for nine minutes. The longer his sermon, the longer he prepares.

Larry says he is not nervous and does not experience mental blocks during preparation or preaching. His primary goal for the sermon is to change the attitudes, beliefs, values, or actions of his listeners. He believes his listeners come to hear him preach because his message is relevant or because the content of the message is what they want to hear; for example, they desire to understand the Bible better, and he explains it well.

Larry's listeners do not talk to him about his sermons, except for cursory "good sermon" remarks at the door. He does not initiate formal or informal processes to encourage such dialogue. Larry's greatest challenge is related to the message, the content of his sermon; he is especially concerned with how to bring fresh insight and relevancy to his content. He correctly discerns that his listeners want relevancy. He does not see his greatest challenge as "fostering relationships with listeners" or "working on his own spiritual life." His education did include coursework on sermon preparation and delivery, which he thinks was adequate. He selects his topics based on a lectionary or by a needs-based topical approach (though he doesn't ask his listeners to delineate their needs).

Larry labels his preaching style: "teacher." Even though he sees his role as teacher, he does not simply supply knowledge; rather, Larry seeks to change his listeners. His preaching delivery is extemporaneous; he uses an outline or an outline with some manuscripted portions. If he is a Protestant, he identifies sermon preparation as his most important ministerial task; if he is a Catholic, his most important tasks are attending to church duties and his own spiritual life. Regardless of his church type, he is not currently spending most of his working time on what he believes to be his most important task. Larry has no role model for his preaching; he does not work to preach like a famous preacher, a personally known preacher, or Jesus.

His listeners' responses are not easily discernible. Larry has had some difficult listeners through the years; for the most part, he is used to looking at many faces that display disinterest. If he is one of the lucky few who has someone with whom to talk about his sermons, that person is probably his spouse or another preacher. With his day to day interruptions, Larry wishes his listeners knew that it takes time to prepare a meaningful sermon. It is a rare week that he has a discussion with a listener about the content of his sermon. Larry truly hopes his listeners know how much he cares about them.

### Mindfulness Minutes ...

(1)   Any surprises?  Make a list of unexpected information from Chapters Three and Four.

(2)   Listeners, preachers, how typical are you?  How are you different or similar to the majority of listeners and preachers in this sermon survey?

(3)   Predict what would happen in your church if the preacher asked a question during the sermon and waited for specific verbal responses.

(4)   Listeners, how would you react if the preacher asked to meet with you to talk about next Sunday's sermon?

(5)   Listeners, have you ever been a difficult listener?  Do you consciously communicate with your face during the sermon?  If not, what kinds of meanings do you think the preacher might attribute to your facial expression?

(6)   Preachers, do you have any behaviors or policies that might discourage listeners from talking to you about the content of the sermon?  Do listeners know the upcoming sermon topics or passages?

(7)   Make a list of the ways you and a partner in sermon communication are similar and different.

## Notes

[1] $F = 5.267$, $p = .024$, t-test
[2] $F=14.897$, $p < .0001$, t-test
[3] $r=.3043$; $p=.003$.
[4] $p=.011$
[5] $p=.016$
[6] $p=.070$, would be significant at .05

Chapter 6

# Let the Dialogue Begin

ELL, PREACHER OR LISTENER, now you know. As partners in sermon communication you have each revealed your leanings and perspectives. While the results of the sermon surveys have been read and those results rest on the previous pages for your future reference, the *understanding* of one another takes more time and effort than the perusal of a few statistics. *Understanding* comes from dialogue.

- Dialogue is conversation in which power is divided equally; to enter into dialogue listeners and preachers must embrace the concept of being "partners" in sermon communication.
- Dialogue includes an imperative for participants to listen so intently that they can summarize the perceptions of the other, they can feel the emotions of the other, and they can incorporate those perceptions and emotions into their own thinking and talking.
- Dialogue requires that participants be open to the examination of their own perceptions in light of the other's revelations.
- Dialogue improves communication competence.
- Dialogue takes time and effort.
- Dialogue actually means "the word *between* us." So dialogue is a conversation specifically designed to increase shared meanings.

## Who Needs Dialogue?

*People with differing perceptions who need to work together.* Mediation in the workplace is a more common phenomenon than it used to be. If co-workers reach a stalemate, or are unable to interact because of differences, productivity and quality can suffer.

*People with cultural differences.* Those who find themselves seated in mediated negotiation sessions often have cultural differences with one other, and often form and maintain perceptions of each others' actions without actually talking.

*People who lack relationship beyond their generalizations of one another.* Trust is lacking because the relationship is surface to non-existent. Stereotyping may be as "deep" as the relationship goes. At a public meeting, one Anglo-American community leader claimed, "All those Asians who want to move here are just planning to start gangs and make trouble. They have no respect for life." It's no surprise that the person who uttered those words is separated by cultural differences from the ethnic group to which he is referring. Do you think he has on-going, frequent conversation with individual human beings from the Asian groups to which he alludes? Well, no—it's not likely. If so, his stereotyped perceptions would receive continual challenge from the lives and words of others.

*People who interpret the behaviors of "the other" through preconceived notions.* Opposing parties see "what they expect to see" given a pre-supposed set of meaning.[1] If I expect you to be hostile to me, and you say, "Good morning!" with a wide smile, I may think, "What a hypocrite. He hates me and he still smiles." If you walk past, pre-occupied, I will interpret that behavior through the same perceptual set, "Oh, you hate me so much you have to pretend like I don't exist." Obviously, many other interpretations are possible, but if I am making meaning based only on my preconceptions, I just reinforce them no matter what you do. Dialogue is one way to alter such a harmful communication pattern.

## Could Listeners and Preachers Benefit from Dialogue?

When it comes to the topic of sermon communication, differing perceptions between preachers and listeners certainly exist.

Since most preachers and listeners don't talk to each other about the sermon, the differing perceptions continue with little challenge. We may be viewing our listeners' behavior or our preacher's behavior through preconceptions. Based on previous experiences, listeners who have come to expect boring sermons get them, because they choose to tune out at the slightest hint of disorganization or irrelevancy. Preachers who assume listeners are not interested will probably notice the listeners with "disinterested" facial expressions. Given such different preconceptions, and the lack of direct discussion, differences can be perpetuated and can serve to diminish shared meanings.

With increasing shared meaning as the goal, it might even be helpful to conceptualize preachers and listeners as being distinct "co-cultures," at least when it comes to perceptions of the sermon. According to the authors of *Communication Between Cultures:*

> We use the word co-culture when talking about groups or social communities exhibiting communication characteristics, perceptions, values, beliefs, and practices that are significantly different enough to distinguish them from the other groups, communities, and the dominant culture.[2]

When it comes to perceptions about the sermon, preachers have much more in common with each other than they do with their listeners. Preachers read the same books, experience the same preparation challenges, have the same occupational stresses, and may talk to each other about preaching from a "sender" approach. Listeners share the experience of listening to sermons week after week. Listeners talk to listeners about sermons. Our perceptions are therefore reinforced by our own "co-cultures."

The organizational system of most churches impedes dialogue between the preachers and listeners. The assumptions that preachers and listeners sometimes make about each other reveal that they may be generalizing, or even stereotyping, rather than actually knowing one another. So, yes, indeed, **dialogue between listeners and preachers could be beneficial.**

We'll get the dialogue started here, and hope it continues in churches between individual preachers and their *specific* listeners. Suggestions for continuing the dialogue are included in this chapter, and every chapter to come.

Many formal dialogues make use of facilitators or mediators who conduct pre-dialogue interviews of all those involved. Those differing perceptions are then summarized and presented to the group before guided verbal interaction begins. Your mediator, Dr. Carrell, will now open the dialogue session between preachers and listeners with a review of your perceptions of the sermon, gathered from listeners and preachers across the United States.

"Welcome to the dialogue. It's great that you've chosen to join the group of listeners and preachers who want to approach the sermon as a communicative partnership. Your efforts will serve to maximize the potential positive, transformative power of the spoken word. How do you all perceive the sermon? Very differently, but let's begin this report with a review of common ground."

## What Meanings Did Surveyed Listeners and Preachers Share?

(1) *The average listener and preacher are aging baby boomers who have just passed the half-century mark.*

Since shared history can aid the process of creating shared meaning in interaction, the match in average age could create the expectation that there is a great deal of shared meaning between preachers and listeners—such as expected speech organizational patterns, historical references, attitudes about morality, parenting approaches, and more.

Such a finding does *not* imply that preachers should target the 51-year-old exclusively! And of course, a mathematical average does not mean that every church fits such a profile; in one church, the forty-something pastor was the oldest person in the church! In another, 80 percent of the church was over 55!

(2)   *Many listeners and preachers agree that sermons should last about 20–22 minutes.*

Listeners and preachers are in agreement about the length of sermons? This finding may send some shock waves through assumption-land. Common connotations about the sermon have listeners lamenting the length as their stomachs rumble and their preachers ramble on and on and on. And on. Yet for Protestants, the 20–25 minute mark seems to be some kind of shared expectation. Let's review the statistics. To the question, "How long should the sermon last?" the answers fell as follows:

|  | *Listeners* | *Preachers* |
| --- | --- | --- |
| Range: | 2–60 minutes | 5–45 minutes |
| Mathematical Average: | 22 minutes | 20 minutes |
| Most Common Answer: | 20 minutes | 15 minutes |

And remember the statistically significant differences between Catholics and Protestants regarding the average ideal length of a sermon:

| Catholic Listener: | 15 minutes |
| --- | --- |
| Catholic Priest: | 9 minutes |
| Protestant Listener: | 25 minutes |
| Protestant Preacher: | 22 minutes |

Says an interviewed preacher, "If you've been boring for half an hour and haven't hit oil, you may as well quit."

Notice that in both Catholic and Protestant churches, the preachers stated a shorter ideal sermon length than the listeners did! Let's remember, preachers reported their perceived "ideal" length, not their usual *actual* length. Being consistent about sermon length is improbable, unless the preacher rehearses orally—and 88 percent of them do not.

Many interviewed preachers report that other components of the service affect the perceived length of their sermon. If a hymn is sung too slowly with more verses than anticipated, Sister Smith has a spontaneous and lengthy testimony, or a youth group "pancake breakfast" announcement is added to the usual service elements, then sermon time is affected. The traditional Catholic service includes more elements than the Protestant service, which may affect expectations regarding homily length. Says one preacher, "The preacher always gets whatever time is left over." Many preachers will take their 20 (or whatever) minutes, no matter what, causing church to get out later even though they didn't preach any longer. Preachers need to be a part of planning the entire service for several reasons, but timing is one of the most important. Conducting an "on-the-spot" editing session has led to increased disorganization in many a sermon—the concluding point, meant to be the climax of the whole sermon, may get axed (or abbreviated beyond recognition) as the preacher tries to make the service cutoff time.

In some "Spirit-filled" traditions, listeners expect that the service and sermon time will vary from week to week. Say some listeners from those traditions:

- "The sermon should take as long as the Holy Spirit needs on that particular morning."
- "Until the message of God has been delivered, we'll keep listening."
- "We had a powerful anointing of the Spirit last week. Many in the church were given a word from the Lord to share. There was no need to be looking at a watch."

Those who expect 45 minutes of preaching aren't likely to shorten their sermons to 20 minutes upon reading the results of this study. Nor should they. What is important is that preacher and listener expectations be discussed, and that the expected time period is honored as often as possible. Showing respect for the listeners with a consistent length of sermon and service can also enable preachers to become more disciplined and better organized. This piece of advice is distinctly different from saying "water it down," "make it trite," "pander to your shallow, antsy listeners who care more for football or dinner than spiritual matters," etc. Shared expectations regarding length remove a distraction ("When is this going to end?") from the listeners mental processing during the sermon.

We should also note that some preachers form their perceptions of what the listeners want based on one vocal listener who sings a continual refrain about the desire for a longer or shorter sermon. Some discussion within the church community will be necessary: What is expected? What has happened in the past? Why does the preacher want 25 minutes to preach? Pleasing everyone is not a tangible goal; however, being consistent about time, well organized, and focused on key ideas are indeed valuable and attainable goals for preachers. Valuable, because the power of the spoken word would be enhanced. Attainable, because communication competence can almost always be increased.

Many, many listeners and preachers, after listing their ideal sermon length answer, added a justification: "Research says that's how long people can listen." Such a rationale was provided for answers ranging from 5 minutes to 45 minutes! Have you noticed how statistics get thrown around and altered sometimes? Especially, when they are separated from an explanation of the research context or even from the researcher's name? Not one respondent included a source for this claim. A few had "heard it somewhere."

In fact, Kenneth Higbee, author of *Your Memory: How it Works and How to Improve It*, claims that listeners can listen with high energy, retaining long-term memories of the presented information, for extended-periods of time (beyond 45 minutes) if they are highly motivated and have at least an average IQ.[3] There are so many variables that affect "how long people choose to listen" that claiming an ideal "cut-off" time for adult attention span is sure to perpetuate fallacies.

How long I am willing to listen depends on many factors. If a two-hour lecture is announced, and I choose to attend to hear a well-known, credible expert talk about my favorite topic with passion, humor, narrative, self-disclosure, and good organization, I will fix my attention on the speaker for the full two hours. I may even say, "My, that went quickly." If, however, a supervisor mandates that I attend a one-hour training session on something I already know how to do, and the trainer is an inexperienced employee who is a disorganized rambler, I will walk out the door (at least mentally) at the 61 minute mark, if not before.

(3)   *Most listeners and preachers agree that the sermon can be prepared in twelve hours or less.*

To the question, "How long does it take to prepare a sermon?" the answers were:

|  | Listeners | Preachers |
|---|---|---|
| Range: | 0–60 hours | 2–41 hours |
| Mathematical Average: | 12 hours | 9 hours |
| Most Common Answer: | 2 hours | 8 hours |

Remember, there is a statistically significant difference between Catholic and Protestant preachers' average hours of preparation.

| Catholic Priest Report: | 3 hours |
|---|---|
| Protestant Preacher Report: | 11 hours |

These data are difficult to decipher with just a glance. The difference in *range* between listener and preacher answers shows us that listeners are predicting rather than reporting, and so are likely to be farther away from the actual preparation time. With a mean of 12 hours of preparation being predicted by listeners and a mean of 9 hours being reported by preachers, we know that many listeners are guessing "high," yet the most common listener answer is "2 hours." Obviously, this is confusing data. That 12-hour "average" is a mathematical average which is being pulled up by about 10 percent of the respondents whose answers were way high (40–60 hours of preparation). Such prep time is not possible, given the other ministerial responsibilities of preachers (not to mention the human need for sleep). Respondents with high answers may have been counting all the hours of a workweek, hours during which a preacher is "living with a text" and in essence, "preparing" for a sermon by processing all of life through the text or topic of the week.

There was no significant difference between Catholic and Protestant listeners' predictions of preparation time. For the Catholic priest, whose parish is typically over 900 members, preparation time for the sermon is much less than for the Protestant preacher whose membership is generally significantly smaller. The priest expects to preach for a significantly shorter period of time and this situation resonates with his perception (shared by 83 percent of his colleagues) that the homily is not the most important part of his responsibilities.

Even with the confusing data, it does appear that many listeners and preachers agree about preparation time, yet the most frequent answer interviewed preachers gave to the question, "What would you most like listeners to understand about preaching?" is "The time it takes to prepare a worthwhile sermon." Why would preachers perceive that most listeners don't know the time it takes to prepare? Many do not (the most common answer was 2 hours), but many of them actually are fairly accurate in their predictions of preparation time, or are even guessing high.

Keep in mind that the number one reason listeners gave for why they don't talk to their preachers is "lack of time" supported by comments such as "preachers are too busy," "she is unavailable," or "the preacher doesn't have enough time to talk to me." Protestant preachers reveal that though the sermon preparation is the most important part of their ministry, they do not get to spend the most time on that task. From the preachers' point of view, as listeners make demands on their time for church meetings, pastoral care, administrative tasks, and other important jobs, it might seem like listeners are insensitive to the time needed for sermon preparation. "All of a sudden they need me at the Sunday School teacher's meeting? I haven't gotten to my sermon yet this week. Doesn't anybody want me to preach around here? Don't they know I need that time for preparation?"

No, they probably didn't know that the preacher needed to prepare at *that* particular time. And if the preacher turns down their request, they may perceive that "she is always hiding in her office" or that "he must not care about Sunday School." The preachers' families can become resentful of the constant demands.

Such common misunderstandings can be minimized. Direct talk is imperative. Open discussion of the responsibilities, schedules, and need for sermon preparation time should be routine. These challenges differ by church size, with the "medium to large congregation with one preacher" model being the most difficult. An organizational "audit" or "review" by an outside professional who makes recommendations about roles and structure may be advantageous in some cases. A beginning step toward understanding can be initiated by preachers in responses they make to requests. Notice the difference between the relational meanings communicated in, "No, I don't have time," or "Yes (but I'll stay up late working on my sermon, dealing with an angry spouse, and resenting you instead of loving you)," or something like, "I won't be able to attend this meeting because several emergencies have taken me away from my sermon preparation time earlier in the week. This is a hard choice because both our sermon and our Sunday School are high priorities in this church. Please send me the minutes of the meeting. I look forward to next month's meeting."

Of course, the "voice" would need to support the warm intent of such a statement. When spoken in a climate of trust and openness, the statement would probably be believed. When spoken in a threatening climate, in which openness has not been the norm, the statement would probably still not be believed. Building a trusting climate takes time; see more about climate in Chapter Seven. Consider this church newsletter note:

*Dear Friends,*

*As you know, I have set a long-term goal of increasing my communication competence from the pulpit. I've discovered that it takes me about three, three-hour periods to study my text, gather supportive evidence, outline, reflect on the input you've provided, rehearse, and revise my sermon. Since I'm a morning person, and mornings are often quiet around the church, I've decided that for the next month, I will block off 7 a.m. to 11 a.m. on Mondays, Wednesdays, and Fridays for sermon preparation. Of course, if there is a crisis in your family on those days between those hours, I will want to be contacted! I'm so pleased that the board has agreed to schedule meetings around my preparation hours. Let's try this schedule for the next month and see how it goes.*

*Remember, my door is always open for drop-in conversation on*

*Tuesday evenings from 6–10 p.m. and if those hours aren't conve-nient for you, just call or e-mail and we'll find a time that works for both of us.*

*One of the most important parts of my sermon preparation is consulting with you.*

*Don't forget the brown bag sermon support group that meets for lunch on Wednesdays from 12 to 1:00 p.m. Bring your ideas, com-ments, and questions. We're working a few weeks ahead: This com-ing Wednesday we'll be discussing Stewardship [or "Please read Mark, Chapter 10, before you come."]. If you can't make it to lunch, be sure to share your input in the Sermon Support Box located outside the sanctuary. We'll include your thoughts in our Wednesday dis-cussion.*

*(4)    Preachers and listeners do not expect substantial pre- or post-sermon talk about the content of the message.*

To the question, "Do you regularly talk to the preacher about his/her sermons?" 78 percent said no, while only 22 percent said yes. Of the 78 percent that said they do not talk to the preacher about the sermon, 64 percent said that the preacher doesn't have time ("is too busy, unavailable," "doesn't want our feedback"); 24 percent felt that it was not their place to tell the preacher how to do his/her job ("I don't want him to think I'm questioning him"); only 12 percent said that their preacher does well, so they didn't feel a need to say anything.

Preachers were asked if they consult listeners as part of their sermon preparation. A full 91 percent do not. It seems everyone is too busy or too entrenched in his or her role expectations. The lack of dialogue is at the root of differences in other perceptions about the sermon. No time? Reorganize schedules, pare down com-mitments, make time. Schedule noontime lunch meetings, evening dessert get-togethers, or Saturday breakfasts for "talking time."

Here's another note from a preacher to her listeners:

*Dear Friends:*
*As you know, I have recently been addressing my problem with workaholism. When I over-commit, my family suffers, my sermons*

*suffer, and my relationships with all of you suffer. Many of you have shared that I seem to be in a hurry most of the time. I know I need to change.*

*To be sure that I have enough time and energy to keep my priorities in order, I am resigning from the Mission Board and the Noontime Lion's Club. Sue Shermans has agreed to take my place on the missions board. While the Lion's Club is an important community connection for me, it is not as important as my other commitments to the church.*

*Instead of my weekly lunch with the Lion's Club, I would like to invite you to bring a sack lunch to the church each Tuesday from noon to 1:00 p.m. so we can enjoy one another's company and some casual conversation. Childcare will be provided.*

*If you have other ideas to assist me, please let me know.*

And here's a suggestion note from a listener to his priest:

*Dear Father:*
*Our church is so big. I've been attending here for almost two years and I am sure you don't know me yet. I'm from a small town and really miss the support that I used to get from my church community, but I come because of your insightful sermons. Sometimes, after a homily, I wish I could ask a question, or that you would have had enough time to discuss life application ideas. Would you ever have time to meet with parishioners, just for lunch or breakfast, to talk about ideas from the homily?*

*Thanks.*

*P.S. I work in technical support at my corporation. If you want to set up an e-mail discussion group, where people could interact about the sermon, just let me know. I'll be glad to help.*

The creation of mechanisms for on-going dialogue about the sermon would bring dramatic change in churches across the country. Suggestions for moving in a dialogic direction are scattered throughout the rest of this book. In general, pre-sermon input and post-sermon content discussion are going to be much more valuable than a weekly post-sermon scorecard: "I'll give him a 7.5 this week; that third illustration was a little biased toward us seniors but his eye contact was better than last week."

Occasional needs assessments ("What kinds of sermons would be helpful?"), demographic inquiries ("What kinds of work are represented in this church community?"), lifestyle questionnaires ("Name the magazines, books, or newspapers you have read in the last month.") and formal dialogue sessions (regarding specific issues in the church) can assist the preacher in knowing the listeners. But no survey will replace the impact of ongoing relationships. *Partners in Preaching* author and preacher Reuel L. Howe reminds preachers:

> ...if he is to be a dialogical preacher it is necessary that he make himself familiar with the meanings that his people will bring to the homiletical encounter out of their experiences. This means that he must become responsive to what they bring, and devise ways in which he can hear and use the laity's potential contribution.[4]

Let's just be sure that the partnership goal promoted by the communication perspective of this book is not reduced to having listeners provide negative critique after each sermon. Please keep reading . . .

*(5)   Listeners and preachers agree that the sermon is important.*
There is agreement between Protestant listeners and Protestant preachers about the importance of the sermon. Remember the most common answer listeners provide for the question: "What element of the service has the most impact on your life?" *The sermon.* And the most common answer Protestant preachers provide for the question: "What is your most important ministerial task?" *The sermon.* For most preachers, this finding should be good news! Sure, listeners still have suggestions, but since they value the sermon, many of them will probably be ready to assist the preacher in making changes.

While Catholic preachers perceive that church duties and attention to their own spiritual lives are significantly more important than either homily preparation or pastoral care, their listeners nevertheless agree with Protestant listeners, rating the sermon as the part of the church service that "impacts my spiritual life the most."

Of the preachers who deliver sermons impromptu, that is, with no preparation beyond topic or text selection, 75 percent are Catholic. For all Catholic priests, the average sermon preparation time is three hours contrasted with the average 11–hour prep time for Protestant preachers. A five-minute homily could be routinely "winged" by an experienced communicator, but priests should note that their listeners are expecting the spoken words of the homily to impact their spiritual life more than anything else in the service. One priest explained the change in perceptions of preaching by saying, "It is not really uncommon now for parishioners to drive to another parish for a visit just to hear an especially good preacher. Just a few years ago, that would have been unheard of in the Catholic church." Says a Catholic listener, "I just can't wait to hear my priest preach each Sunday. He feeds my soul." Don't forget that one of the priests' top priorities corresponds with the listeners' advice: attending to your own spiritual life. Perhaps from a deepened spiritual life, the impromptu preparation procedure allows inspirational, insightful, life application to flow. The sheer numbers of parishioners in most Catholic churches drastically impacts the number of hours needed for pastoral care, weddings, funerals, etc. One campus-based Catholic priest routinely performs 70+ weddings per year! Perhaps the traditions of the Catholic Church cause some priests to perceive that the homily is of less importance than their other church duties. Their listeners disagree. So does Andrew Greeley. In his book, *How to Save the Catholic Church*, Greeley asserts:

> Unlike Protestant ministers who, knowing the central importance of their preaching, spend many hours preparing their Sunday sermons, most Catholic priests do little homily preparation. Many rely on a stock set of ideas largely unrelated to issues important in the lives of the congregation. Even some priests who do spend time preparing their homilies do so in a vacuum. For

> them, revelation is one-dimensional, the Church
> and Scripture its sole sources; people are exhorted
> to love God, to be followers of Christ, to preach
> the Kingdom, but there is little mention of how
> this is to be done.[5]

It is interesting to note that Catholic and Protestant listeners agree about lots of things: good and bad sermons, reasons they listen to sermons, typical reactions to sermons, whether or not they can recall something they gained from a specific sermon, the impact of the sermon on their spiritual lives, and the advice they have for preachers. When it comes to preaching, their only area of disagreement has to do with length.

To return to the dialogue: "Preachers and listeners, I've described and investigated the meanings you do share with each other, actually uncovering differences embedded in some of the apparent similarities. Now, let's shift the focus to your lack of shared meaning, your distinct perspectives."

## What Meanings Do Preachers and Listeners Not Share?

*(1)   Most preachers are men; a majority of listeners are women.*
A majority of listeners are female (61 percent) and an overwhelming majority of preachers are male (84 percent): this gender difference has important implications for the listeners' relevancy plea. A thorough discussion of gender differences in sermon communication would produce its own multi-volume text. Most public communicators are careful about pronoun usage and illustrations, but there are broader concepts needing our consideration if we are to more thoroughly understand how gender differences can affect communication. One of the most important of these gender-related concepts is what we call *disconfirmation*.

"No one is going to talk to you or look at you for the whole recess." Such a playground punishment was worse than a good thrashing! Being ignored, being treated as though you did not exist . . . being "disconfirmed." Interpersonal communication scholars tell us that such treatment is worse than overt spoken negativity.[6] How can you recognize disconfirmation when you see it? If you speak in a meeting and I continue the meeting as if your words were never spoken, I disconfirm you. If you are listening, and I speak as though you are not there, I disconfirm you. Unfortunately, disconfirmation of women is common in the sermon communication of many male preachers. Male preachers, does your language communicate as if "from one man to another?" Then, according to those of us who study human communication, it disconfirms more than half of the people who are listening. And I'm sure you don't intend to do that. Disconfirmation is not a component of competent communication.

For many female listeners, this gender difference contributes to their perceptions about sermon irrelevancy and the preacher "not really knowing them." Sometimes, attempts by male preachers to be "inclusive" are limited to illustrations that include, but trivialize women. For example, one retired minister hired to preach in a small church routinely referred to women in condescending ways. Of course, he did not intend to put women down, but, nonetheless, he did make frequent statements, from the pulpit, like,

- "I attended the women's group meeting and they actually let me get a word in edgewise."
- "Some of those modern women, those working women libbers, don't understand the meaning of the word *mother*."
- "After you women make up the beds of a morning, and the family is all gone off to school and work, when you have some time on your hands—you may want to take some of that time to thank God for each of your children."

While most of the listeners in the church were women who worked inside and outside their homes, they kept their irritation to themselves. Why?

- "We're a small church. This is what we can afford."
- "He's never listened to other people's feedback."
- "I'm sure he wouldn't get it."

Remember Chapter Three, "Rethink These Please?" We have to get past the notion that intent is everything. Because he has no intention to put down or exclude women, a male preacher might think, "I'm not biased against women. How could anyone think such a thing?" But bias is frequently non-intentional; bias can simply display our lack of understanding about something. Of course, many do argue that male bias is more commonplace and intentional in the church than in other cultural institutions, such as schools or corporations where male bias has gone underground. In church traditions that believe in male-only leadership, disconfirmation may be used to reinforce male authority. If so, then any request from a woman for "inclusive language" or sermon illustrations that demonstrate respect and understanding of women's lives, may be seen as "threats" to the male leadership policy rather than as legitimate requests for increased relevancy. In the process, it is possible for the sermon to lose relevancy and connection for women.

Recently, one church on the West Coast decided to hire a "women's minister." A woman who interviewed for the position said the interview was a short one: "They described my role as 'teaching women how to be submissive to their husbands; how to be better homemakers.' First, I mentioned that all women are not married. Then I let them know that I would be encouraging every woman to discover her spiritual gifts and grow in her faith. Imagine, a team of men who believe a 'minister to women' should focus entirely on that one idea. Their trivialization of the spirituality of women was appalling."

Reveals another listener, "I was told in private by the preacher that my 'rational' nature was so unusual for a woman; he also wished out loud that his deacons could be less emotional—after all, he said, that's why we use men as deacons so emotional issues don't cloud our judgment. He wanted his church full of women who were homemakers only because that's the 'spiritual way' for women to be. Obviously, I felt unwelcome, silenced, even though he said what he had to say in a very kind tone. Lots of my friends who have chosen a season of working at home also resent his condescending attitude about women. It's like he thinks we're less complex than men or something. Like, he's preached Proverbs 31 and the submission verse, so he's done his duty for women this year."

Now most gender disconfirmation is not so blatant. When intentional, it is the antithesis of the Christian gospel; when unintentional, it may be simply the male preacher's tendency to speak from his own experiences (like we all tend to do). A male preacher's "default" would be to pick illustrations that resonate with his own experiences. If he is married, he might routinely label the spouse in a story as "a wife." If he is a sports buff or literature lover, he will pick illustrations and quotations that reflect those preferences because he finds them meaningful.

But all public communicators, male or female, have a responsibility to include evidence that will be meaningful to listeners, not just to themselves. The disdain some preachers display toward issues related to "political correctness" and issues raised by "radical feminists," can make it difficult for them to think clearly about gender differences and communication. But if preachers are going to be "messengers of God" to more than 39 percent of their congregations, they will need to wrestle with and resolve these issues.

Says one preacher, "There is a significant group of women in my church who believe God wants them at home. I don't want to 'disconfirm' them or other women who choose to work or have to work outside the home." According to Martha C. Ward, author of the text, *A World Full of Women* (which could be very helpful to male preachers who are actively trying to understand the perspectives of women), women and men both work:

> Here is an amazing fact: Everyone from conservative male sociobiologists to radical Marxist feminists agrees that the sexual division of labor is fundamental to being human . . . At the same time, these people do not agree on *why* the sexual division of labor is true. Some say God, religion, nature, science, or mothers make us live this way . . . The basic point to understand here is that all women work. All mothers and wives have jobs. That these may be invisible or un-rewarded is immaterial. That they may be acknowledged or ignored, easy or life threatening, is totally beside the point. Women still work.[7]

Speaking as though listeners are all male is a habit for some male preachers. Using male-centered or condescending illustrations is also routine for some. But the discussion of gender issues in the church should not be limited to talk about pronouns and anecdote characters, or arguments about women's work or role expectations. The issue is an issue of disconfirmation. Not disagreement, but the silence of behaving as if the perspective of women does not exist, or that their perspective is trivial. Disconfirmation is behavior that communicates: "You don't matter." Disconfirmation and trivialization of women is an issue for the male-dominated preaching profession to thoroughly investigate.

For example, "domestic abuse" absolutely permeates our culture. In fact, "Psychotherapist Carolyn Holderread Heggen maintains that conservative religiosity combined with traditional role beliefs is the second-best predictor of child sexual abuse—second only after the use of drugs or alcohol by the father."[8] And yet, according to many surveyed listeners, the topic is rarely broached from the pulpit by male preachers. The silence about this perceived "women's issue" communicates volumes. Is physical, emotional, and mental abuse of women and children okay with the church? "Of course not," some of you are thinking, getting a little irritated with your author as you remember that weeping woman who sat in your office just last week. Well, silence from the pulpit about such issues does "communicate" a lack of compassion, whether intended or not.

*Christianity Today* recently reported on "The Ecumenical Coalition on Women and Society," a group of Christian women who have determined to bring the international problem of abuse of women and children to the attention of the Christian church.[9] My question? Why doesn't the issue already have the attention of the Christian church as a whole? Echoing listeners in this sermon survey research, executive chair of the World Evangelical Fellowship Commission of Women's Concerns, Winnie Bartel, asks, "When have you ever heard a pastor preach on abuse against women and children?"[10] Moving away from debating issues like ordination and leadership roles, the group has determined to "make a difference in the world."[11]

Most preachers are men. A majority of listeners are women. Ignore it. Chew on it. Explore it. Discount it. Trivialize or capitalize. A communication perspective will insist, if preachers and listeners are to be partners in preaching, that the issues related to gender difference must be accepted as real. And, we must struggle to overcome them.

*(2)   Most listeners think preachers are nervous yet more than half of preachers say they are not.*

Since most people in the general population experience some degree of communication apprehension,[12] listeners are probably projecting their own feelings of public speaking apprehension onto their preachers. In other public speaking contexts, listeners can't accurately discern which speakers are experiencing nervousness.[13] The error of those listeners in other public speaking contexts is that they assume speakers are not nervous, even when speakers report that they are nervous.

Most public communicators don't display their nervousness in a way that is detectable to their audience, but a majority of speakers report feeling apprehensive. So what is it about preachers that causes more than half to report that they are not nervous? A group of Protestant preachers at a recent gathering suggested:

- preaching weekly diminishes nervousness; the context becomes comfortable
- they are "called" to be preachers, which gives them confidence
- perhaps they're accepting a degree of competence that is adequate and habitually "easy" for them rather than challenging themselves to higher degrees of competence or variety in their sermons
- maybe they are not aware of nervous mannerisms which listeners might be detecting[14]

*(3)   Preachers and listeners have different goals for sermon communication time.*

Let's review the statistics on these expectations.

| Preachers: What is your general goal when you preach? | | Listeners: Why do you listen to preaching? | |
|---|---|---|---|
| Change the listeners | 54 percent | Inspiration | 35 percent |
| Translate from text to today | 17 percent | Life application | 30 percent |
| Inspire | 13 percent | Information | 21 percent |
| Transmit information | 11 percent | Insight | 14 percent |
| Don't know | 4 percent | | |

- Preachers: 65 percent of your listeners want either inspiration or life application. Says one long-time preacher: "Every sermon should be inspirational."
- Fifty-four percent of preachers want to change the listeners. And what about their sermon communication partners? Well, when surveyed listeners were asked, "Why do you listen to sermons?" not even one listener identified "a desire for change" as the reason they come to the sermon. However, an assumption could be made that since 35 percent of listeners want to be inspired and another 30 percent want life application—an inspiring sermon with life application suggestions could activate a desire to change. Nonetheless, listeners can generally be classified as "apathetic" to the preachers "change" goal since they do not attend with the expectancy that they will be changed. Though surveyed listeners did not identify their listening goal as "I want to be changed," when the listener survey posed the question, "What is your inner reaction to most sermons?" 14 percent of listeners reported that their typical inner reaction is "a readiness to change." Remember, one of those listeners admits, "Sometimes he kicks me right in the bum." While virtually all of this 14 percent speak of personal, interior changes, *one* listener mentions change that has an outward result. The type of change suggestions to which listeners respond seems to be the type of change that coincides with the individualism of the broader, dominant culture. An urban preacher from the East wants to counter this self-focus, saying he longs for a

post-sermon comment like: "That was really hard hitting. Now I'm going to give everything away and move to Calcutta."

- Though only 17 percent of preachers hope to serve as "translators" between the Scripture and the listeners, 30 percent of listeners say they attend sermons hoping for "life application" possibilities, "translated" meaning. Yet only 15 percent of listeners report that their inner reaction to most sermons is, "That was relevant to daily living." Rather, when asked, "What is your inner reaction to most sermons you hear?" one surveyed listener spoke for many when he replied, "After most sermons, I'm left asking 'What about me?' "

- Thirty-five percent of listeners come for inspiration; 13 percent of preachers list "inspire" as their general goal.

- Fourteen percent of listeners want insight; no preachers mention providing insight as a goal (though 17 percent of preachers want to translate the text to today's Christian).

So, should listeners change their expectations or should preachers change their goals? Perhaps the better question to ask is: "Should they affect each other, forming collaborative sermons which include listener and preacher perspectives—sermons which both challenge and affirm, which inspire and inform, which are relevant while still motivating change in listeners?" In reality, *that* is the question we should answer.

(4)  *Preachers have misconceptions about what listeners want from a sermon.*

When interviewed preachers were asked, "What would you like listeners to understand about preaching?" the third most common response was: "We wish the listeners had more basic Bible knowledge." Interestingly, one listener gave the following piece of advice to preachers: "The homily is about the only chance most of us get to hear from the Bible each week. Make sure we do." In addition, the call to preachers to "Keep the content Scripture-based or God-centered" was indeed loud and clear. These perceptions reinforce one another: Listeners expect preachers to provide the

Scripture for their week; preachers want listeners to take more personal responsibility for their own spiritual lives. The degree to which listeners take responsibility for their own spirituality will probably be determined person by person, yet the sermon which provokes thought and inspires reflection is more likely to motivate listeners to become more active in their own spiritual growth than the sermon which "provides the answers."

Another difference of opinion between listeners and preachers has to do with the notion of "entertainment." Says one preacher: "My difficult listeners *just* want to be entertained. They expect the pastor to offer illustrations, have enthusiasm, and really draw the person in." And my question? Is a conversational and passionately delivered sermon that includes relevant illustrations "entertainment" or competent communication?

Listeners did not ask for amusement, but they did ask for relevant illustrations, enthusiasm, and connection. Perhaps listeners and preachers have different meanings for the word "entertainment." Listeners think, "Can't we have good public speaking and a relevant, spiritual message?" while some preachers think, "If I have to offer illustrations, display enthusiasm, and draw the listener in—I am denigrating the message." To the contrary. For preachers with this "don't entertain" perspective—think about this question: If better organization and better delivery enable your listeners to better internalize your intended message, doesn't working on those processes actually serve your specific purpose?

Another preacher connotation regarding "entertainment" is that "inspiration" is merely entertainment. Notice how inspirational writings like *Guideposts,* the poetry of Maya Angelou, and inspirational television shows like *Touched by an Angel* are so popular. In a cover story, *People* magazine described *Touched by an Angel* as a show which "dispenses comforting homilies," actually "saving lives" with its communication of meaning about God's love, hope, and peace.[15]

Notice that 35 percent of listeners attend the sermon for *inspiration.* Is that need for spiritual uplift the same as a desire for entertainment? No. In fact, listeners crave depth. They call it insight. Of course, perceptions of "sermon depth" may differ among preachers and listeners. So what does depth mean? A young adult listener at a recent retreat suggested there are different levels of profundity: from intellectual depth, to philosophical depth based on logic, to the kind of depth that comes from personal experience, to the creative depth of a "new angle on an old story."[16] One preacher characterized his sermons as occasionally "too deep" for listeners because of the "complex logic" of a theological concept which compelled him to structure a presentation with numerous main points and sub-points as well as to include many detailed Greek and Hebrew translation explanations. Perhaps listeners are looking more for the kind of depth that comes from lived experience (that spiritual depth 17 percent wanted their preachers to pursue) or that "creatively insightful" kind of meaning, in which the preacher finds a new way to interpret a familiar text. Says one preacher with admirable understanding, "You have to dig deep to get simple again."

If listeners wanted "just entertainment" they could stay home and be amused by professionals whose humor is bouncing around space to satellites in their own backyards. Rather, they want well-presented, spiritually-centered depth. Indeed, listeners may need to become less passive in their role to garner the greatest gain from the sermon, but the differing interpretations of entertainment and depth must be considered by the preacher as well. Furthermore, preachers who still believe listeners' primary desire is for "entertaining" sermons should note that it is the preachers who seem more concerned about delivery than their listeners; 35 percent of preachers name some aspect of delivery as their greatest challenge while 78 percent of listeners do not mention any aspect of delivery when describing a "good sermon."

Let's summarize what we have learned from each other.

## What Listeners Want Preachers to Understand

Provide a relevant message with clear ties to Scripture. Foster relationships with listeners. Work on your own spiritual life. Work on your organization. Work on your delivery. You are appreciated.

## What Preachers Want Listeners to Understand

It takes time to prepare a worthwhile sermon. The message is from God. We wish the listeners had more basic Bible knowledge. They need to know they can trust us. They need to think for themselves. Every sermon cannot be a masterpiece. Most preachers would preach themselves to death if someone encouraged them.

## Let's Talk

Now that we know the similarities and differences in perceptions of preachers and listeners regarding the sermon, let's begin a dialogue.

Preacher: I'll start with an important point. The message of the sermon is from God.

Listeners: Then be sure it's God-centered and linked to Scripture. Deepen your spiritual walk. Be sure your sermon delivery reflects that deep walk with God. Demonstrate insight that reflects your spiritual life.

Preacher: How do you decide how deep my spiritual life is or is not?

Listeners: It shows in your sermons. When you do the same thing, the same way, with the same message all the time. When your voice sounds like you don't care about the message or us listeners.

Preacher: How's *your* spiritual life? The sermon is supposed to assist your spiritual life, not *be* your spiritual life. I wish my listeners had more basic Bible knowledge.

Listeners: We want you to be sure your key points are linked to the Bible. Show us the relevance of the Bible to our lives and maybe we will read it more.

Preacher: Okay, but I still wish you would spend more time reading, reflecting, and thinking about your own faith. Move beyond what happens in the sermon. You need to think for yourselves.

Listeners: Show us with the sermon that Scripture is connected to our daily lives. Show us how your faith has brought you practical insight. Inspire us. The more irrelevant the sermon, the less likely we will be to read the Bible on our own.

Preacher: It seems like you don't trust what I say sometimes anyway.

Listeners: Have you read the newspaper today? We hear a lot about preachers who can't be trusted. Do you know what happened with our last preacher?

Preacher: I will just keep doing my best to show you that you can trust me. I am doing my best with my sermons. There is just too much to do. Have you ever tried to preach? Every sermon cannot be a masterpiece.

Listeners: We are looking to the sermon for spiritual meaning in our lives. We are really expecting that the preacher and the sermon be as perfect as humanly possible.

Preacher: That's not ever going to happen. I'm going to make mistakes and get tired and overwhelmed, just like everyone else.

Listeners: Well, okay. But we still wish every sermon could be a masterpiece. At least, we wish for inspiration and life application. We wish for you to know us, have a deep faith, and demonstrate that depth in the sermon. We want your sermon to be well organized so we can leave with the key idea still in our heads.

Preacher: I have too much to do to prepare that kind of sermon for you every week.

Listeners: But the sermon is so important to our spiritual lives.

Preacher: Are you willing to give me the time to prepare more thoroughly?

Listeners: Don't you have time on your hands? What could you possibly be doing all day?

Preacher: Here's my "Seven Habits of Highly Effective People" time management day planner. Look at last week. Thursday and Friday tasks didn't get done because of the tragedy in the Smith family.

Listeners: We didn't even hear about that until Sunday. We could have helped. Do most of your weeks look like last week?

Preacher: I work about sixty hours a week. I usually just fit in sermon prep between all the meetings and emergencies. I have one day off. People who call on that day of the week have complained that "Pastor's not available for us."

Listeners: Well, what do we need to do?

Preacher: I need time for sermon prep. I need time to deepen my own spiritual life.

Listeners: We had no idea you were being asked to do so much.

Preacher: I'm not Billy Graham. I can't keep up with Hollywood.

Listeners: We don't want anyone else. But we do want and need your best sermons almost every week. Let's work together to find a way to help you make preaching your top ministry priority.

Preacher: I'll preach myself to death if you all begin to encourage me.

Listeners: You seem pretty sure of yourself. Do you really need our encouragement?

Preacher: Yes.

Listeners: Do you just want positive feedback, or do you want to hear the entire set of meanings? What if we have something to say that isn't positive?

Preacher: I want to know that you are tuning in, thinking about what I say. If you have to be negative, I hope you'll be gentle, but I still want to hear it.

Listeners: You don't act like you do. You always seem to have the right answer. Just walking up to you out of the blue with a suggestion would take more guts than most of us have. You don't provide any way for us to just talk about sermons.

Preacher: There isn't any time.

Listeners: Oh, that again. Well, preaching is your job. If you don't care for our perceptions, that's okay. So if we tune out your sermons for the rest of our lives, is that okay too?

Preacher: No.

Listeners: Well?

Preacher: Some of the things you want are not things I want to give you.

Listeners: What do you think we want?

Preacher: Entertainment. Brevity. Easy, warm fuzzy messages that reinforce that you should just stay the way you are.

Listeners: That's a little insulting. I could stay home and get better entertainment.

Preacher: But you want the sermon to be relevant, inspiring, and connected to your lives.

Listeners: That's not entertainment. That's competent communication. That's what Jesus did with his listeners.

Preacher: You *do* want my sermons to be shorter.

Listeners: If you'd preach the length you said was "ideal" in this study, we'd all be satisfied. What we really want is a meaningful message—with a key point we can find. We really hate it when you ramble on and on to unrelated tangents. Better organization is more important than less time. Sometimes it just seems long because we can't follow you.

Preacher: What about the easy, warm fuzzy messages of affirmation?

Listeners: Life is really challenging sometimes. We want affirmation and inspiration from our faith. An uplift, not a put down.

Preacher: If I just affirm you all the time, you'll never change. I want you to change.

Listeners: Change is hard. Love more. Give more. Pray more. Serve more. I've heard those. I need to know how to love my arrogant boss. I want to give my money to truly needy people. I say the Lord's prayer daily. I'm on a church committee.

Preacher: The mediator is whispering to me that we should both check out Section Four.

Listeners: One more thing. Please don't read to us.

Preacher: Only 13 percent of us do.

Listeners: Then give us eye contact please. When you look at your notes so much, we feel like you are talking at us, not with us. Make it seem more like a conversation.

Preacher: I don't want to make a mistake or forget anything. I've been doing it this way for a long time and nobody ever said anything.

Listeners: You never asked.

The Mediator, Dr. Carrell: We're out of time for today, but I think we've gotten a good start here. Perhaps you can set up a process and some time for further dialogue.

Well, now. That was a nice dialogue. Of course, since it was fictional, understanding, illumination, and empathy came early and often! "Superficial and sappy," some are saying. Changed attitudes and actions came too easy. Indeed, change is hard for any system, any individual. But we need to start somewhere. How can preachers and listeners work toward increasing their sets of shared meaning about the sermon? For further progress toward that goal, let's leave the mediation moment, the dialogue table, and spend some time eavesdropping on people who study other face-to-face public communication contexts: teaching and (the most overlooked communication concept of all) listening.

# Notes

[1] Wolvin, A., & Coakley, C.G. (1996). *Listening* (5th ed.). Boston: McGraw Hill.

[2] Samovar, L.A., Porter, R.E., & Stefani, L.A. (1998). *Communication between cultures* (3rd ed.). Belmont, CA: Wadsworth, 50.

[3] Higbee, K.L. (1988). *Your memory: How it works and how to improve it* (2nd ed.). Englewood Cliffs, N.J.: Prentice Hall.

[4] Howe, R.L. (1967). *Partners in preaching: Clergy and laity in dialogue.* New York: The Seabury Press, 84.

[5] Greeley, A.M., & Durkin, M.G. (1984). *How to save the Catholic church.* New York: Viking Penguin, Inc., 189.

[6] Devito, J. (1986). *The communication handbook.* New York: Harper and Row.

[7] Ward, M. (1996). *A world full of women.* Boston: Allyn and Bacon, 3–4.

[8] Hancock, M. & Mains, K. B. (1997). *Child sexual abuse: Hope for healing* (revised ed.). Wheaton, IL: Harold Shaw Publishers.

[9] Gardner, C.J. (1999, April). "Women resist abuse globally." *Christianity Today,* 20.

[10] See *Christianity Today.*

[11] See *Christianity Today.*

[12] Motley, M.T. (1988, January). "Taking the terror out of talk." *Psychology Today,* 46–49.

[13] Carrell, L.J., & Willmington, S.C. (1998). "The relationship between self-report measures of communication apprehension and trained observers' ratings of communication competence." *Communication Reports, 11*(1), 87–95.

[14] Carrell, L.J. (workshop facilitator) (1999, April). *Listening to our listeners.* Anchor Pastors Retreat, Warrenville, IL: Chapel Ministries.

[15] (1999, February 2nd). Cover Story: "Touched by an angel." *People,* 88–89.

[16] Fulmer, L. (workshop participant) (1999, April) *Listening to our listeners.* Anchor Pastor's Retreat, Warrenville, IL: Chapel Ministries.

# SECTION 3

# TIME
# TO
# LISTEN

*"Hollering doesn't make a person hear any better.
It just hurts our ears."*

A LISTENER

Chapter 7

# The Preach as a Teach

**T**EACHER.
What does this word mean to us?
Educator.
Instructor.
Schoolmaster.
Professor.
Coach.
Preacher?

Preaching is indeed a *unique* face-to-face public speaking event. Yet it is not *so* unique that it has no overlap with other types of human communication in other contexts. For example, so many surveyed preachers claim, "I am really a teacher," *not*, "I am a little bit like a teacher sometimes." It is loud, clear, and definite: *I am a teacher.*

Preachers also had lots to say about "difficult listeners" and listeners had plenty to proclaim about preachers who are not exemplary listeners either. Says a listener, "My preacher makes it quite clear that he is not interested in listening to us though he certainly expects us to listen to him." Said one preacher, "One of my most difficult listeners proclaims with his whole body, 'I'd rather be somewhere else and I'd rather you be somewhere else.'"

Researchers have long been studying communication competency in teaching and listening. Since sermon interaction has great overlap with these communication competency areas, taking the time to listen to relevant research findings and pragmatic suggestions regarding teaching and listening, will be time well spent. Remember from Section Two that when preachers are asked to "Choose a word or short phrase that best describes your preaching style," the number one response is: *Teacher.*

Teaching and preaching do have a lot in common. Though only 5 percent of preachers name Jesus as their role model, it is still worthwhile to note that Jesus was called "Teacher" by his disciples. What *lessons* can we learn by exploring the *preach* as a *teach*?

Some similarities are obvious. Front rows stay vacant in church and classroom until latecomers are forced to fill those conspicuous seats or pews. Collections are taken, property taxes are assessed, tuition is billed. The teacher and preacher are paid for their work. We believe that they should have something to offer us. Another similarity? Listeners let preacher and teacher know that it is time to finish—by shuffling bulletins or notebooks, or even with the (presumably inadvertent) noontime beeping of watches.

Some differences are apparent as well. In most churches, a raised hand and verbal request are not necessary for restroom respites. Though perfect attendance awards may be given in elementary classrooms and Sunday School, attendance becomes more choice-driven for adult students and sermon-listeners. We come because we want to hear what will be said, or because we know we need to be there.

By comparing preaching and teaching, are we reverting to the notion that preaching is mostly about "transmitting information"? While some assume that the primary role of a classroom teacher is to get facts into the mind of the student, most educators expect to be doing more than that. In 1998, educators from 183 countries formulated this vision statement for higher education:

> Ultimately, higher education should aim at the creation of a new society—non-violent and non-exploitative—consisting of highly cultivated, motivated, and integrated individuals, inspired by love for humanity and guided by wisdom.[1]

Education is potentially transformative. And certainly, the goal of the sermon is transformation as well. In this study most preachers who identify with a "teaching" style agree with other preachers: The primary objective of their preaching is to *change* the listener.

As first graders learn about phonics, they gain more than discrete bits of information such as "The silent 'e' at the end of a word makes the first vowel say its name." This information is not an isolated fact intended only to be memorized and regurgitated. As cumulative concepts are understood and applied, they allow the gradual development of literacy. Students learn to read! Students are informed, but also motivated, inspired, and given insight. Once they learn to read, then they can read to learn. Transformational? Of course!

Try to remember the best teacher you ever had. Do you recall simply the information shared by the teacher, or more? Did she care about you? Was he inspiring? Did she notice your potential and encourage its development? Was the classroom a place where you mattered? This exercise often results in a list that includes many of the following remarks:

What do teachers say when asked to describe their best students?

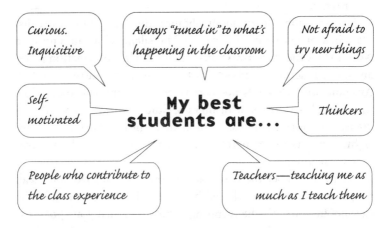

Examining research that describes good teachers and good students will be a helpful extension of our thinking about sermon communication. What we want to do is to remember the *partnership* mandate; teaching and preaching are communicative. Not sender to receiver, but interactive, simultaneous, co-creation of meaning. Not monologic, but dialogic! As we look for linkages between preaching and teaching, we must keep our focus not on teachers or students exclusively, but on the product of their interaction: *learning*.

Certainly, the similarities between preaching and teaching end at some point. Teachers in most classrooms are not praying, relying on the Holy Spirit, or using a Biblical text. But, at the adult level, teachers are informed by a text and grounded in a foundational theory, need extensive class preparation, want their learners to be changed by the learning, and recognize that student motivation is necessary. So what are the most obvious differences between the teach and the preach?

Generally, teaching is more interactive than preaching. Many who educate adults routinely use interactive pedagogical techniques, such as small groups, open discussion, case studies, and other "active learning" strategies. The not as common as it used to be "lecture" approach to teaching is most closely associated with typical sermon preparation and delivery. Perhaps this paradigmatic shift in higher education (from a "teacher as informer" focus to a classroom interaction "learning" focus) will also take place in preaching. As the discerning reader has likely concluded by now, the communication perspective offered in *The Great American Sermon Survey* suggests that changes that increase interaction between preacher and listener are desirable.

In educational contexts, formal assessment is the norm. Assignments, papers, tests, and grades are part of life for students everywhere. Such direct measurements of learning are rare to non-existent after a sermon. The assessment is not up to the preacher, but perhaps, some interviewed preachers suggest, up to God. The assessment occurs in daily living choices, the private life of the mind and soul, and spiritually motivated social action. Some traditions have begun to stress "accountability"—to other Christians or to a spiritual mentor, but not through preacher-formulated, overt assessment. While the grade a student receives on the Graduate Records Exam (GRE) can well change the rest of the student's life, many Christian preachers would remind us that the final spiritual assessment has eternal ramifications.

So, though the overlap between *the teach* and *the preach* is not complete, there is enough in common between the two processes to warrant a closer inspection. As people interested in sermon communication, we must all sit up and take notice. As we preachers and listeners examine the results of research related to learning in educational contexts, we can be on the lookout for ideas applicable to our own roles as communication partners during the sermon.

So dim the lights in the sanctuary—listeners, imagine the smell of chalk, the institutional paint color, the shuffling and creaking of other students' chairs, the weight of your backpack as you slip into the last remaining seat. And preachers, imagine yourselves with lecture notes ready, watching the black, round clock staring at you from the back wall, wondering who has read their assignment, and feeling comfortable with the vital content you'll be sharing during class . . . . Now, let's bring up those lights in the classroom-sanctuary as we try to illuminate the *preach*, as a *teach*.

## Teacher Communication Competence

We can each remember our great teachers. We can also remember those who were not so great. The powerful effects of their teaching are a part of us. Remember the "Good morning future garbage men of America" comment from Section One? The daily repetition of that comment to an eighth grader in 1968 "inspired" my husband, Cliff Carrell, to become a middle school educator with a vastly different approach, a person who has made a *positive* difference in the lives of literally hundreds of students!

Keeping your personal experiences in mind, let's move from the specifics of your classroom learning to summaries of research on the topic. Our question? What are the communication characteristics of teachers who best facilitate learning?

A recent national survey of secondary teachers, principals, and university education faculty concludes that the following criteria are deemed appropriate for evaluating the effectiveness of teachers: preparation for class, classroom control, enthusiasm, ability to motivate students, public speaking skills, interpersonal communication skills, the ability to actively involve students, and the creation of a positive climate.[2] Another education scholar provides a shorter list of criteria for evaluating teacher presentations to adults: expertise, empathy, enthusiasm, and clarity.[3]

Still further research provides the following findings:

- There is an association between the concept of "ideal instructor" with one who participates, gives approval, accepts differences, and demonstrates sincerity and understanding.[4]
- Students at secondary and collegiate levels rate clarity, rapport, and effective delivery as communication behaviors of effective teachers.[5]
- When student and teachers share a similar style of learning, they perceive one another more positively.[6]
- A dramatic communication style, which is energetic, attention getting, and humorous, is also linked to effective teaching.[7]

Generalizations from the research in "Communication Education" generate the following consistent characteristics of teacher communication competence: immediacy, clarity, creation of a supportive classroom climate, and attention to student differences. Though the wording may differ, many of those research-derived effective teaching criteria overlap with listener-perceived effective preaching criteria.

Why are these communicative characteristics identified as effective, competent, and even excellent by teachers and students? Because they foster learning. Because they create the possibility for transformation.

## Immediacy

The most consistent finding related to excellent teacher communication is a set of communicative behaviors that has been termed *immediacy*.[8] Great teachers are "immediate" communicators. This term does not mean that teachers who enable learning always begin and end class on time! Nor does it mean that they can answer questions a spilt second after you ask them. Rather, immediacy has been defined as "The teacher's use of communication behaviors that enhance physical and psychological closeness" among teacher and students. [9]

Immediacy behaviors are divided into two sets: verbal and nonverbal. Verbally immediate teachers use spontaneous humor and verbal praise of students' ideas. They also follow up on student-initiated topics and demonstrate that they are willing to have conversations with students outside the classroom.[10] Nonverbally immediate communicative behaviors are approach behaviors, signals of availability, which communicate interpersonal closeness and warmth. Such behaviors are displayed consistently through multiple channels; for example, eye contact, vocal expression, and body movement.[11] The "multiple channel" caveat ensures that students are able to discern the sincerity of immediacy behavior; "fake warmth" is generally detectable through the contradictory messages displayed through competing channels.

For example, while teachers may make overt requests for dialogue which appear verbally immediate ("This is confusing material. If you have any questions, I'll be in my office until 5 p.m. today"), their classroom communication can scream other negative relational messages through nonverbal behavior that is not immediate. If students' comments are squelched in class, the same students won't believe that the invitation for dialogue after class is sincere. If a brusque and hurried manner are the norm for the teacher's oral delivery, then students will be less likely to speak up, fearing the reaction.

Preachers who want listeners to become more responsive will also need to be aware of the verbal and nonverbal "non-immediate" relational messages they communicate. Listeners say...

- "He asks for feedback all the time but those who have tried to talk to him just get a brief, not very nice, explanation of why he believes he is right. His reputation for not tolerating those who disagree is well known. If you question him, his smiles, his handshakes, his questions about your life, all change. I wouldn't dare tell him what I think, even in a kind, roundabout way."
- "He is so sure of himself that I can't imagine he's receptive to other points of view."
- "I shared my ideas about preaching in a casual conversation and he took it as a personal insult. I think he is a great preacher, but he thought that because I had some thoughts about preaching I must be dissatisfied with his preaching. I heard through the grapevine that he thinks I am probably going to leave the church. The rest of us take criticism at work all the time—we get evaluated and sometimes we set goals for improvement."
- "Any comment ever given is met by a paranoid, defensive response. The person who tried to give the comment then gets prayed for or once he even said something from the pulpit about how 'some people think this' and how he's praying for them. Of course, we all knew who he was talking about."
- "Preachers are so used to believing they are right about everything, so sure of themselves. How can you approach one to talk? Their way of being shuts us all up and we just pretend everything is perfect."

Learning to give and receive constructive criticism can be difficult, especially for people in positions of power (like professors and preachers) who are used to being perceived as "the authority" on their subject. Immediacy requires openness, but does not negate leadership. Listening intently without interrupting, asking questions for clarification, withholding judgment and defensiveness for the first responses—are all communicative skills necessary for receiving constructive criticism.

Students most frequently rate "teacher immediacy" without conscious awareness; they don't use communication education jargon terms like "immediacy." But for the teacher effectiveness research, students do complete evaluation tools like the *Immediacy Assessment Instrument* created by researcher Dr. J. Gorham.[12] Gorham's *verbal* immediacy instrument asks students to rate the frequency (from "never" to "very often") of the following teacher communicative behaviors: self-disclosing, asking questions, using student ideas in class, using humor, knowing and using students' names, conversing with students before and after class, using personal pronouns such as "we" when talking about the class, caring about students' feelings and perceptions, and providing both praise and criticism. The *nonverbal* immediacy assessment instrument allows students to evaluate teachers' vocal expressiveness, facial expressiveness, gestures, eye contact, relaxed body position, movement around the classroom, and use of culturally appropriate touch.[13]

After perusing this list of immediacy behaviors, some preachers may be thinking that displaying immediacy is just a mechanism for winning a popularity contest; but the growing body of immediacy research goes well beyond saying that students *like* teachers who are immediate. Indeed, we have definitive evidence demonstrating that students *learn more* from teachers who are highly immediate. Immediacy is linked to student motivation.[14] Motivated students pay attention better in class.[15] This heightened energy given to listening aids memory.[16] And so on. In addition, from the research in communication education, we know that immediacy behaviors for teachers are important because immediacy combats the effects of gender difference, at least with some populations.[17] Say researchers Anderson, Edwards, and Jensen "The positive effects of immediacy in the classroom have been firmly established."[18]

It is my hypothesis that displays of preacher immediacy create the same positive results in the sanctuary.

Can immediacy be faked by teachers or preachers? Can a public communicator get away with contradictory attitudes and actions? "I hate these lazy students who don't read their text, but since I'm being evaluated today I'll send verbal and nonverbal messages of warmth, acceptance, interpersonal closeness, and availability for communication." Do you think the students will buy the facade? The answer is no. Such attempts at deception will usually be detected by students who can discern that your words may be warm, but your tone is not, or that your eye contact and your posture reveal a contradictory message.

Preachers, it's time for a little sifting. Get out those cautionary sieves. The communication education researchers are *not* suggesting that you *pretend* to be immediate. Immediacy is a behavioral demonstration of a teacher's attitudes and beliefs such as: students matter, the classroom process needs to be interactive, this content is valuable, my students are partners in learning, my students deserve respect, etc. Certainly, beginning teachers may need to learn to overtly display their "immediate" beliefs and attitudes. Such a case is different than saying, "Get out from beyond the lectern (or pulpit) and walk around so they think you like them and want to be 'close' to them, even though you don't."

Remember the advice listeners provide for preachers in *The Great American Sermon Survey*? Two of the major suggestions from listeners are suggestions potentially related to immediacy, suggestions that not even one preacher identified as a primary challenge.
(1)  "Foster relationships with listeners. Be real. Preach with us, not at us."
(2)  "Work on your own spiritual life. Be genuine. Display your depth and sincerity."

We listeners will discern through the preacher's verbal and nonverbal behavior whether or not we are viewed as partners in interaction, and whether or not the preacher cares for us as individual human beings. Communicators can learn to better reveal their authentic attitudes of immediacy.

It might appear that becoming more immediate can be accomplished by smiling a little more and using a listener's life experience story in the sermon once in awhile. Not bad ideas, actually, but from the listener perspective and from a communication education perspective, immediacy needs to come from the "inside out" to be believable, to be ethical. For preachers to increase their immediacy, they need to build those relationships with listeners. An honest desire to know listeners is requisite.

Preacher, do you actually believe that the listener is a partner in sermon-communication? Are you moving away from the monologic model? If so, we listeners are likely to perceive you and your preaching as increasingly "immediate." We probably won't use the term, but we will be more motivated, we will pay better attention, we will increase our mental participation in the sermon interaction, we will look for ways to move from being passive to being active, and we will learn more.

## Supportive Classroom Climate

In the northern regions of the Midwest, springtime is usually a painful process. When temperatures climb to the upper thirties and the sun peaks out from behind the seemingly terminal grayness for a moment in early March, some newer residents spout cheery greetings like, "Spring's coming!" while those who've been around awhile grimace, muttering mild expletives. Hopes are usually dashed with frigid temperature dips, heavy April snows, and buds which refuse to do their budding until Wal-Mart's "Spring fashions" are swapped for sand shovels and swimsuits. This is called the *climate*.

Certainly, climates differ. For Easter, a discouraged northern climate dweller has only to travel straight south for a few hours to find blooming dogwood and redbud trees, and sweatered churchgoers complaining that "it's not supposed to hit 70 degrees for another week or two." Climates differ. And all those who wait for spring know that the daffodils and forsythia need the right climate to grow.

So do human learners.

When growth is the goal, learning climates matter in the

classroom. And the church. When the signals of spring are tardy, we long for a change in climate. Like the enduring icicles of a spring in the north, physical discomfort, embarrassment, frustration, boredom, and fear signal that the classroom climate is not yet ready to support growth, to enable learning.[19] How do we know the climate is right for growth?

Pamela Cooper, author of *Communication for the Classroom Teacher,* reminds teachers that "The best means of facilitating learning is to create a positive classroom atmosphere."[20] Cooper identifies supportive classroom climates as those that are characterized by:

- openness rather than defensiveness
- confidence rather than fear
- acceptance rather than rejection
- trust rather than suspicion
- belonging rather than alienation
- order rather than chaos
- high expectations rather than low expectations[21]

Listeners, preachers—does the sermon communication in your parish or church create this kind of climate? Who is responsible for climate? Preachers in churches with less than supportive learning climates may blame negative listeners while listeners may point the finger at the preacher's communication patterns. If students have to "sit through a dull teacher presentation, one that is repetitive, boring, insufficiently challenging, banal, platitudinous, or too easy,"[22] the classroom climate can become aversive to learning, can become that late spring freeze that kills off the newly sprouted crocus. If listeners' responses are difficult to decipher, inauthentic, passive, continually negative—preachers will perceive a difficult learning climate.

Once the teacher behaves in ways that produce an aversive climate, students can engage in self-fulfilling prophecies, behaving as if the class is sure to be boring or that it will always be irrelevant or non-challenging. They may respond from a fear framework, or may have to worry about dodging public putdowns. Their responses to teacher climate behaviors will create a perpetual, negative spiral as teachers respond to student expectancy cues. The truth is that aversive classroom climate is reciprocal, and both teachers and students need to work to make changes.

Says Lenora Tisdale in her insightful book, *Preaching as Local Theology and Folk Art*,

> The preacher, on the one hand, is a dance partner . . . On the other hand, the preacher is also charged with the task of imaginative choreography . . . At its best, the Sunday morning sermonic dance inspires others, making them want to put on their own dancing shoes and join in the steps of faith.[23]

Because the preacher is perceived to have the most power in the interaction, the listeners can easily say, "If it's going to change, *he* needs to change it." But, imagine that the listeners are so enthused about the potential for joy in the dance that they determine to raise their listening energy, even if the preacher hasn't altered his preaching at all.

Says one preacher about the call and response "dance" of his African-American preaching tradition, "They move me. When I come in tired or preoccupied with a worry, with a just 'okay' sermon going, their energetic responses energize me. As I'm energized, my preaching gets better and better."

Or perhaps the preacher begins to ask less than responsive listeners to bring in stories related to next month's sermon texts or topics. Will the use of the listeners' stories change the dance? The point is partnership, our shared responsibility, our communicative dance. As "they" have said, "It takes two to tango." Teachers and students, preachers and listeners, together, in their contexts, create and sustain climate.

Certainly anything that affects learning climates negatively can create low expectancy, which in turns fosters more negativity, diminishing the possibilities for growth. Have you seen this happen in church? Some climates are chilly when the new preacher arrives. Others become chilly when sermons don't offer relevance, inspiration, or insight. Or when the preacher unintentionally says something that, given the history of the church, is perceived as "wrong" or "offensive." The preacher may have a vague sense that something is wrong, but the church culture, and even the climate itself, may keep him from getting a current "weather report." One minister went about his business in a chilled climate for two years before the deacons called a meeting to ask for his resignation over something he had said 24 months prior. No one had spoken to him about the incident at the time. We must all accept our responsibility for the climate.

The roles of teacher (and preacher) can set up climate rules for students (and listeners). Some of those rules can diminish honest dialogue. Some of those rules may diminish immediacy. In the adult classroom, open discussion of ideas is more common than open discussion of classroom process, evaluation methodologies, or teacher behavior. Dialogue with the teacher regarding class process is generally held in private; the degree to which one can challenge the teacher's ideas in class is generally prescribed by the teacher.

In church, the "rules" about challenging the preacher are often even more restrictive. We can clearly conclude from *The Great American Sermon Survey* that church climate does not typically "allow" for preacher-listener conversation about the sermon. We've all admitted it. While students may be afraid for their literal grade, pew-persons may be afraid for their figurative grade:

- "What will she think of me if I don't understand why she talks about 'works' most Sundays and then preaches a sermon on 'grace' that implies works don't matter?"
- "If I mention that his illustrations are usually male-centered or that they promote stereotypes about women, he'll think I'm some kind of 'radical feminist'—whatever that means. I know he doesn't like them."

These rules restricting interaction need to be reconsidered in some classrooms and some churches, if we are to move toward the goal of a more supportive learning climate co-created by both listeners and preachers.

## Clarity

How do teachers know when they have accomplished the goal of *clarity?* When their students *understand* what is being taught. That's right. Clarity cannot be judged by teachers' perceptions of their own behaviors. Clarity is a product of the interaction. Back to Section One . . . clarity is evident when shared meaning is created in the minds of teachers and students. What does communication education research tell us about clarity?

- Ratings of teacher effectiveness in many settings are based largely on the concept of clarity.[24] Without clarity, teachers are not competent communicators.[25]
- Teacher clarity is related to student achievement.[26] When students understand content and process, their grades and accomplishments reflect that understanding
- Teacher clarity is related to teacher verbal and nonverbal immediacy.[27] Displaying immediacy can assist teachers with the goal of clarity.
- Regardless of student age, teacher clarity is perceived in similar, positive ways.[28] Whether students are in elementary or graduate school, they want and need clarity.
- Clarity is not an ambiguous concept. We can identify communicative behaviors that demonstrate clarity including using concrete examples, providing practical applications, varying voice to emphasize key ideas and conceptual linkages, repeating complex ideas, and incorporating a variety of types of supportive material from multiple perspectives.[29]
- Students' responses affect the level of teacher clarity.[30] Learners have power to incite teacher clarity with their nonverbal response behaviors (for example, looking confused) and with direct questions (for example, "I don't understand how you got from point three to point four").

Students leave every class session with some conscious or unconscious rating of their teacher's clarity:

- "I think I understood everything that happened in class today. I just need to review, remember, and link the concepts to related portions of the text."

- "These assignment instructions didn't make sense to me. And where was she going with that 'immediacy' thing?"
- "Why wouldn't she give us a specific answer about the length of this research paper we're supposed to write?"

At the end of a course, or as part of a research procedure, adult students may be asked to *formally* rate teacher clarity. One of the most recent instruments used for that purpose was created by Cheri Simonds (1997) and includes evaluation of teacher process clarity and content clarity. In general, teachers with high clarity are teachers who use specific and concrete language, avoid tangents, preview coming tasks, include relevant examples, provide practical application of concepts, summarize content, and explain expectations explicitly.

How can we plan for high levels of clarity? As a professor, I begin course planning with a lengthy list of general goals for the course. My next step is narrowing and focusing those general goals into student-centered behavioral objectives that are used to guide my preparation. Before I ever outline a lecture or structure an assignment, I must have a clear view of what I want students to be able to do as a result of their learning. Writing such listener-centered objectives would be a great aid to preacher clarity.

Those who are first learning to write behavioral objectives make two frequent types of errors. "The teacher will draw a rectangle on the board to show the difference between a rectangle and a square." The first common error? That statement tells us what the teacher will do, not what the student should be able to do as a result of the lesson. To help pre-service teachers overcome that error, we educators teach them an acronym "SWBAT"—Students will be able to . . . ." So then pre-service teachers will write, "The student will be able to learn the difference between a rectangle and a square." Second common error? Using a vague verb like "learn" in a behavioral objective. What will they do? How will we know they have "learned"? Behavioral objectives need to lead us to assessment. They need to be "behavioral." While students learning to write behavioral objectives may perceive that the professor is just picky about wording, the wording (as usual) is important because of the educational philosophy it connotes. Is the lesson about what the teacher will do to the student, or what the students will be able to do as the result of the lesson?

Preachers can set behavioral objectives for their lessons; not "I will provide an informative sermon on the divinity of Jesus," but rather,

- "After this sermon, listeners will be able to identify three characteristics of Jesus' life that demonstrate he was fully human and fully divine."
- "After this sermon narrative entitled 'Lost and Found,' listeners will be able to orally explain the connection between the emotions of the main character in the parable and emotions they have experienced in a situation of loss."
- "After this series of sermons titled 'The Praxis of Compassion,' listeners will be able to commit to one of the three community service projects the church has organized."

"Student" centered. Behavior centered. A lesson for preachers from teachers? Clarity of instruction needs clarity in planning. Let me repeat, **a clear lesson is a result of goal-directed lesson planning.**

Constructing behavioral objectives is a helpful mental discipline for preachers as they plan sermons. What is your goal? What is it you want listeners to know and be able to do as a result of your sermon? To help you remember, try using the acronym LWBAT.

Within lectures and units, teachers high in clarity include previews, direct statements that link previous learning with new concepts, internal summaries, transitions from one concept to another, looping of concepts to previous concepts, and repetition of complex topics presented through a variety of mechanisms. Many concepts must be taught again and again, and teachers must employ multiple methods of reinforcing previously introduced skills. Teachers in training are often asked to be able to explain the same concept at least three different ways. For instance, can you think of three ways to explain why 3 x 3 = 9? Most any third grade teacher could. Clarity—for students—is the goal.

Obviously, most second graders "understand" first grade lessons, but they are not ready to teach first grade because they cannot communicate first grade content in ways that their younger friends can understand. If a first grader says, "I don't get it" after the teacher completes her lesson on primary colors, the teacher does not recite the same words again in the name of clarity! Rather, the teacher finds another way of helping the student think about the same material. That's the teacher's job. In the same way, that's the preacher's job too.

Of course, some teachers do just pull out yellowed notes to read, some teachers perceive their role as "tellers" rather than facilitators, and some students cheer when early retirement plans urge such teachers on to other endeavors. And some learners pass to the next grade or even frame a diploma without having met the behavioral objectives. Teachers and preachers must pursue clarity.

## Learner Differences

"What's your style?" is the nineties version of the sixties pickup line, "What's your sign?" Taking some sort of a short quiz, which puts you in a "style" category, can be a fun form of self-analysis. Of course, many popularized style instruments are simply a set of questions someone dreams up. Women's magazines are notorious for including argument-inducing surveys which are supposed to determine some kind of "relationship style." "Find out if you and your man are really a match!" read a recent cover of a popular magazine read by millions. A few years ago, *Glamour* magazine published a personality style explanation based on the shape of one's lipstick after several applications! Beyond such silliness, there are theory-based, literature-related, research-supported style assessments that are widely used in educational circles.

A style is a learned pattern of learning behavior that makes sense to the person who uses it; there is not one best style.[31] Teachers all across this country have become aware that there are differences in the ways in which people process information. Remember that teacher who used to say "My way or the highway"? Such teachers are not common these days, as most teacher training programs include lessons in learning style. Many adults in the general

population have become intrigued with the notion of style as well—
"discovering" that your difficulty in school may have been related
to your "kinesthetic learning style" butting heads with a teacher's
"auditory style," rather than a lack of potential or IQ, can be a
freeing moment. Underlying the style movement in education is a
premise: Educational practices which take student style differences
into account enable better learning. Learning style groundbreakers,
Guild and Garger, challenge educators:

> The study of style should be a positive reminder
> of the reason most of us chose to be educators—
> the challenge of helping individual students to
> reach their full potential. The implementation of
> style is a joyous celebration of diversity.[32]

What is learning style? Learning style research focuses on the
ways through which learners prefer to receive information. The
three learning styles include auditory ("Do you learn best by hearing?"), visual ("Do you learn best by seeing?"), and kinesthetic/
tactile ("Do you learn best by experiencing?").[33]

Auditory learners enjoy speaking aloud. Said one auditory
learner: "If I can talk it out, I understand." And another, "If I hear
it explained, I won't forget it." Auditory learners often assume
everyone appreciates discussion as much as they do. If they are
teachers, and they've given you an oral instruction, auditory learners
expect that you will remember it because they would remember it.
You can imagine that speech communication departments are full
of professors with auditory learning styles.

Visual learners can be easily annoyed by teachers who are teaching primarily to auditory learners. A graph, an image, or an object
can be extremely helpful aids to memory for the visual learner. A
teacher who provides a sentence outline on a transparency, the
same outline on a handout, and then lectures though the outline is
not servicing the needs of multiple learning styles; in fact, the listeners are *less* likely to process and remember content because
they don't have to participate mentally. Visual learners will learn
best if they can graphically organize ideas. While graphs, charts,
and objects can be appropriate additions to orally presented

material, using language to create visual images in the minds of the students (or listeners) is highly recommended as well. Visual supportive evidence should not duplicate spoken words, but rather enhance, augment, and support spoken words. Remember Jesus speaking to visual learners—the lost coin, the mustard seed, the lamp that should not be covered.

Most teachers are able to combine visual and auditory styles more readily than they are able to incorporate the kinesthetic/tactile style on a regular basis. On the first evening of a graduate school class called "Brain Research," I (an auditory learner) was ready to take notes and then to find a study partner with whom to discuss the material. I knew I could learn all the medical terminology if I spoke it aloud over and over. Much to my horror, that first night of class, my professor distributed bowls of fruit—kumquats, oranges, bananas, grapes, avocados, and toothpicks, asking us to "build a brain out of fruit." I was humbled to failure and my kinesthetic professor made an important point that has stayed with me to this day. If all my education had been kinesthetically-oriented, I would never have made it to grad school so easily in the first place! Her challenge to my preferred auditory learning style taught me lessons about teaching that I use to this very day. The current educational system does favor auditory and visual learners; kinesthetic learners are often labeled "behavior problems" because they prefer activity to sitting quietly in their desks.

Traditional preaching favors the auditory learner as well. How can preachers work to reach those with kinesthetic learning styles who are seated in the pews each Sunday? One such listener describes his preacher's approach. "He recently did a sermon on the idea of 'Take Ten.' He gave us each ten dollars. We were trustees of the money. What would we do? I am stunned by how I had not been seeing my money as all belonging to God anyway."

*Stunned?* Now there's a post-sermon comment preachers don't hear too often. Just think about how tactile Christ was—offering a drink of living water; using the boy's small lunch of loaves and fishes to feed the crowd; asking the man healed of paralysis to "Get up, take your mat, and go home" in full view of them all.[34] Doing demonstrations, which can become analogies for spiritual concepts, is a viable approach. Simulations, dramas, projects, and "hands-on" materials are tools for tactile learners.

One of the reasons for the effectiveness of "narrative" in preaching and teaching is that it provides an excellent mechanism for addressing visual and kinesthetic learning styles while presenting information orally. In his excellent book, *First Person Preaching*, Daniel Buttry proclaims,

> The drama of a good story can grasp the hearers and transform them. The drama has the power to stimulate feelings, thinking, and action. It then becomes the igniter of new drama, moving from the story of the tale to the story unfolding in the hearer's life.[35]

While fully 39 percent of surveyed preachers say they use stories as supportive evidence on a regular basis, the other 61 percent of preachers might wish to take a workshop in the oral art of storytelling, allowing themselves to be videotaped and critiqued by a professional. To induce creativity and insight, a preacher might job-shadow a listener, and then re-write a Biblical parable into that work context.

As part of their study of the text, preachers need to brainstorm visually and kinesthetically, recording every sight, sound, touch, smell, and taste of a scriptural setting. The tight, slow shove through the crowded, narrow street on the way to Golgotha; the feel of sweaty bodies pushing against yours as you strain to see Jesus; the smells of the open market, of panic, of the mob mentality; the sounds of children crying and Jesus moaning in pain; the sight of gashes on his back . . .

At the very least, preachers should check their verbs, adjectives, and adverbs to be sure they appeal to more than one of the senses. Preachers, ask yourself, is there anywhere in this sermon where listeners will be prompted to create a vivid image in their minds? Says David Schlafer, author of an article titled "Preaching as Sacred Play,"

> The preacher's Scripture text must be teased and tussled with *as a vigorous presence*, rather than

check-listed as a set of sedimented deposits. The text must be read aloud—over and over, in different translations—preferably acted out. Better yet, it should be read aloud and acted by a group of very diverse people; after which follows a discussion, not about the 'meaning' or 'the point,' but the questions, the curiosities, the sensory stimuli it kicks off for different reader-hearer-actors. This process of playing with the text, is of course, far from disrespectful. Rather, it is granting a living and active word, which Scripture focuses for us, the respectful hearing it deserves.[36]

Auditory-geared preachers, remember that kinesthetic learners "actually learn better when they touch and are physically involved in what they are studying."[37] Visual learners learn best when they can see an image or object or graphic organizer that serves as an illustration. "Let me feel it, experience it, and then I can understand. Let me see it to believe it." These statements represent valid paths to learning.

For preachers, who are, of course, educators, the examination of learning style differences should lead you to three significant generalizations. If you do nothing else with learning styles, at least consider the following:

### Know your own learning style

Self-awareness is imperative. This knowledge will support your growth toward increased communication competence. Your listeners are sure to have a variety of styles. It is important to balance "playing to your own strength" with "being sensitive to the learning style differences" of your listeners. Remember, research has demonstrated a match between teacher and learner is related to perceptions of excellence they may have of each other.[38] Those who are your closest supporters may be listeners whose learning style matches your own. Consequently, it is essential to gather the input and responses of listeners whose styles do not match your own so you can broaden your understanding of how you are perceived. And you must remember that their comments are not "negative"; rather, they are just coming from a different way of learning. Accepting those differing learning styles as "real" can actually be exceedingly freeing and exciting once you get the idea.

### Use a variety of preaching methods

Surveyed preachers say that getting fresh ideas is a challenge; sensitivity to the variety of learning styles can freshen learning for the entire congregation. Our fall back approach for preaching and teaching will generally be related to our own style. It takes awareness and rigorous work for an auditory learner to employ kinesthetic methodology. When changes are attempted, the preacher should feel free to openly discuss them. Tell your listeners why you are doing what you are doing; not change for the sake of change, but change based on the fact that in our church community we have people who learn spiritual truth in all different ways. Referring to the connection between teachers and students and style, Simon and Byram wrote a book with an apt title for teachers and preachers, *You've Got to Reach 'Em to Teach 'Em.*[39]

### Develop an appreciation for style variety

A good way to do this is to listen to other preachers as often as you can. Several listeners report hearing preachers denigrate other preachers—preachers with different styles. A few even observed such a phenomenon occurring during a sermon; for example, one listener describes the following situation: "A preacher whose sermon style had been criticized by a parishioner or two became entrenched in his belief that his style was actually more spiritual than others styles. From the pulpit, his negative references to other styles of preaching included mention of specific preachers and implications that listeners who appreciated other styles were not as strong in their faith as they should be."

Were the other preachers preaching heresy? No. Doctrinal differences were actually minimal in this case, according to the listener reporting the story. How could this happen? Well, it seems to be possible for well-intentioned, deeply spiritual people to begin to believe that almost *all* of their perceptions are God-driven and thus, the only "correct" perceptions. Another preacher remarked that preachers defending sermon style "X" *were flat wrong*. Interestingly, in interviews, three preachers with completely different communicating styles all stated that Jesus was their role model for preaching. Perhaps Jesus provides a teaching style model that works because it reaches all of us.

Exposure to a wide variety of preaching styles is remarkably eye opening. We may act from our own styles, assuming they are The Best, rather than one of a variety of valid approaches. Treating the learners as communication partners means preaching in ways that are best *for a variety of learners* rather than preaching in the way that may have become comfortable for us over time. So become a humble learner at the feet of other preachers. Learn how they connect to their listeners and ask, "Can I adapt this idea to my situation?" Adding variety to your preaching style is recommended, even though it can be difficult.

"I am a teacher," say so many surveyed preachers. Indeed, in the classroom-sanctuary, there is much for preacher-teachers and listener-learners to reflect upon. Immediacy, clarity, supportive learning climate, and attention to learning style differences are necessary for effective teacher communication, and, if pursued by preachers, could create dramatic transformations in their sermons.

Lessons from communication education research lead us right back to a dialogic format. Indeed, Jane Vella, author of *Learning to Listen, Learning to Teach* (and other magnificent adult education texts), uses stories of powerful teaching from all over the world to support her contention that "adult learning is best achieved in dialogue."[40] The monologue approach to preaching and the principles of effective teacher communication are like antagonistic magnets, repelled from each other, impossible to push together.

Can you almost hear Jesus talking to preachers? "Once there was a teacher, in a great classroom, with learners gathered to hear the Word . . ."

Create your own parable using immediacy, clarity, climate, and learning style to pursue the partnership-preaching paradigm. Where does it take you, preachers? Listeners? While not many preaching traditions are ready to move to an open discussion format for sermon time, there is a path that leads away from monologue in the direction of dialogue. Let's follow it, together.

# Notes

[1] Declaration of the World Conference on Higher Education (1998, October). "Higher Education In the Twenty-First Century: Vision and Action": Paris.

[2] Johnson, S.D., & Roellke, C.F. (1999). "Secondary teachers' and undergraduate education faculty members' perceptions of teaching-effectiveness criteria: A national survey." *Communication Education,* 48(2), 127–138.

[3] Wlodkowski, R.J. (1985). *Enhancing adult motivation to learn.* San Fransciso, CA: Jossey Bass.

[4] McGlaughlin, M.M., & Ericson, K. (1991). "A multidimensional analysis of the ideal interpersonal instructor." *Communication Education,* 30, 397–398.

[5] Cooper, P.J. (1995). *Communication for the classroom teacher* (5th ed.). Scottsdale, AZ: Gorsuch Scarisbrick Publishers.

[6] Carrell, L.J. (1991). "Cognitive and spoken language style relationship." Doctoral dissertation, University of Denver.

[7] Norton, R. (1983). *Communication style: Theory, applications, and measures.* Beverly Hills, CA: Sage.

[8] Anderson, J.F. (1979). "Teacher immediacy as a predictor of teaching effectiveness." In D. Nimmo (Ed.), *Communication Yearbook 3* (pp. 543–559). New Brunswick, NJ: Transaction Books.

[9] Gorham, J., & Christophel, P. (1990). "The relationship of teachers' use of humor in the classroom to immediacy and student learning." *Communication Education,* 38, 46–62.

[10] Gorham, J. (1988). "The relationship between verbal teacher immediacy behaviors and students learning." *Communication Education,* 37, 40–53.

[11] See Anderson.

[12] See Gorham.

[13] Plax, T.G., Kearney, P., McCroskey, J.C., & Richmond, V.P. (1986). "Power in the classroom VI: Verbal control strategies, nonverbal immediacy, and affective learning." *Communication Education,* 35, 43–55.

[14] Menzel, K.E., & Carrell, L.J. (1991). "The relationship between preparation and performance in public speaking." *Communication Education,* 43, 17–26.

[15] See Cooper.

[16] Higbee, K.L. (1988). *Your memory: How it works and how to imrpove it* (2nd ed.). Englewood Cliffs, N.J.: Prentice Hall.

[17] Menzel, K.E., & Carrell, L.J. (1999). "The impact of gender and immediacy on willingness to talk and perceived learning." *Communication Education*, 47(1), 12–20.

[18] See Anderson, K., Edwards, C., & Jensen, K.K. (1999, April). "Examining the relationship between verbal immediacy and teacher clarity in the college classroom." Paper presented at the joint annual meetings of the Central States Communication Association and the Southern States Communication Association, St. Louis, MO, 5.

[19] Civilky, J. (1982). "Self-concept, significant others, and classroom communication." In L. Barker (Ed.). *Communication in the classroom* (pp. 161–162). Englewood Cliffs, NJ: Prentice Hall.

[20] See Cooper, p. 200.

[21] See Cooper, p. 2.

[22] See Cooper, p. 201.

[23] Tisdale, L.T. (1997). *Preaching as local theology and folk art.* Minneapolis, MN: Fortress Press, 93.

[24] French-Lazovik, G. (1974). "Predictability of students' evaluations of college teachers." *Journal of Educational Psychology, 66,* 373-385.; and Murray, H.G., & Lawrence, C. (1980). "Speech and drama training for lectures as a means of improving university teachers." *Research in Higher Education,* 13, 73–90.

[25] For example, see Cooper; Cruickshank, D.R. (1985). "Applying research on teacher clarity." *Journal of Teacher Education,* 36, 46–48; and Wlodkowski, R.J. (1985). *Enhancing adult motivation to learn.* San Francisco: Jossey Bass.

[26] Frey, P., Leonard, D., & Beatty, W. (1975). "Student ratings of instruction: Validation research." *American Educational Research Journal,* 12, 435–447.; and Hines, C.V., Cruickshank, D.R., & Kennedy, J.J. (1985). "Teacher clarity and its relationship to student achievement and satisfaction." *American Educational Research Journal,* 22, 87–99.

[27] Sidelinger, R.J., & McCroskey, J.C. (1997). "Communication correlates of teacher clarity in the college classroom." *Communication Research Reports,* 14, 1–10.; and Powell, R.G., &

Harville, B. (1990). "The effects of teacher immediacy and clarity on instructional outcomes: An intercultural assessment." *Communication Education*, 39, 370–379.

[28] See Hines, Cruickshank, & Kennedy.

[29] See Powell, & Harville; See Sidelinger, & McCroskey; McCaleb, J.L., & Rosenthal, B.G. (1983). "Relationships in teacher clarity between students' perceptions and observers ratings." *Journal of Classroom Interaction*, 19, 15–21; and Simonds, C.J. (1997). "Classroom understanding: An expanded notion of teacher clarity." *Communication Research Reports*, 14, 279–290.

[30] For example, Berliner, D.C. (1976). "Impediments to the study of teacher effectiveness." *Journal of Teacher Education*, 27, 5–13.; Berliner, D.C. (1987). "Simple views of effective teaching and a simple theory of classroom instruction." In D.C. Berliner & B.V. Rosenshine (Eds.). *Talks to Teacher* (pp. 93-110). New York: Random House.; Perry, R.P. (1985). "Instructor expressiveness: Implications for improving teaching." In J.G. Donald and A.M. Sulliven (Eds.). *Using research to improve teaching* (pp. 35–47); and Kendrick, W.L., & Darling, A.L. (1990). "Problems of understanding in classrooms: Students' use of clarifyfing teactics." *Communication Education*, 39, 15–29.

[31] See Carrell, 1991.

[32] Guild, P.B., & Garger, S. (1985). *Marching to different drummers*. United States: ASCD Publications.

[33] Dunn, R., Dunn, K., & Price, G.E. (1975). *Learning style inventory*. Lawrence, KS: Prices Systems, Inc.

[34] Mark 2:11–12; *New International Version*. Grand Rapids, MI: Zondervan Bible Publishers.

[35] Buttry, D.L. (1998). *First person preaching: Bringing new life to Biblical stories*. Valley Forge, PA: Judson Press, 7.

[36] Schlafer, D.J. (1996). "Preaching as sacred play." The College of Preachers Fellowship Paper 101, 7.

[37] See Guild and Garger, 63–64.

[38] See Carrell, 1991.

[39] Simon, A., & Byram, C. (1997). *You've got to reach 'em to teach 'em*. Dallas, TX: Training Associate Press.

[40] Vella, J. (1994). *Learning to listen, learning to teach*. San Francisco, CA: Jossey-Bass, Inc., 3.

# Chapter 8

# Listening to the Preacher

**L**ISTEN TO MY WORDS," says the preschool teacher at least a dozen times as she encourages the children to transition from their play time to the next activity. As Anita sits down for story time, the teacher congratulates her, trying to motivate the others.

Anita, I like the way you have listened to my words. You are sitting down. You are waiting for story time. Nice job. Who else is listening to my words? Good, Ahmed. Yes, Stephen. Good listening. Jack? Sophie? It's time to sit down on the mats for our story. Good listening Sophie. Katana and Miranda, Cheyenne, Yolanda, good listening. Jack? Jack. Listen to my words. Jack?

Listen to my words. Not just hear them, *listen* to them. The teacher, gently urging, with soft tones, and kindness, (and no doubt a high level of immediacy!) repeats the direction again and again, asking the children to "listen to my words." There is an implication in her instruction. If you listen, you will obey. If you listen, I will see the response.

As we age, we learn to do all kinds of listening. Appreciatively listening to music. Listening to an explanation of a new life skill. Serving as friend, listening to a heartbreak, and empathetically, sharing the pain. Dissecting persuasive attempts—not just obeying, but listening analytically, coming to our own conscious conclusions.

And, we perfect Jack's skill—tuning out. We learn how to look like we're listening, when we are not. We learn that listening is a process we can turn off or on at our own discretion. We become aware than some speakers make it easier to listen than others do. Sometime, somewhere, during the process of maturity, we may conclude that the listening choices are occurring automatically, that we are not *selecting* a listening energy level, but rather that we have become either poor listeners or good listeners.

We find that our response, the behavior that demonstrates our listening, affects our communication partner. How long will that amiable pre-school teacher wait for Jack?

First of all, there is an important distinction to be made between hearing and listening. It is, after all, a big difference. Hearing is the *automatic* process of the auditory system. Stimuli are "received" through the aural receptors. "Whereas hearing is the ability to receive the sound vibrations that are transmitted, listening is making sense out of what you hear." [1]

An estimated 28 million U.S. citizens have hearing impairments.[2] These hearing impairments affect listening, often leading to an increased reliance on visual perception. The listener in this study whose one piece of advice for preachers was to get a better sound system probably needs amplification so he can hear. As he said, "If I can't hear you, it doesn't matter what you say." Listening relies on the physiological functioning of the auditory system. Efforts of churches to provide amplification devices and interpreters who translate spoken English into American Sign Language are on the increase. But millions of us without *hearing* deficits, do indeed have *listening* deficits.

Say the CB-using truck drivers, "Got your ears on?" Well, listening takes more than having our ears attached—we must also turn on our minds. Hearing is automatic, and the challenges are generally not within our control. Listening is voluntary, a set of behaviors involving our choice. While low IQ affects listening ability, an average or high IQ doesn't guarantee good listening.[3] To be sure, plenty of smart folks are poor listeners.

Perhaps the greatest listening deficit is a duet of attitudes:

(1) "The speaker is responsible for my listening effectiveness."
(2) "My role as a listener is a passive role."

If you hum this duet as you "listen" to a sermon, you diminish the potential power of the spoken word. Why bother to come? Sure, the preacher should adopt behaviors that motivate you to choose to listen with high energy, but what is *your* "should"?

"Showing up," say some listeners. "I am giving the preacher the opportunity to do his job."

As listeners, our power extends far beyond the tune in, tune out option. As media consumers, we often take the "viewer" approach, the viewer with limited power. "I'll show NBC! I'll just channel surf during this extended period of commercials. Of course, I'll have to keep checking back to be sure I don't miss one second of *ER*."

Our listening capabilities take us well beyond channel surfing. Given a communication perspective, listening is not the process of sitting silently awaiting the receipt of the sender's message. Listening is an active, choice driven set of skills that benefits from conscious attempts to concentrate, improve memory, evaluate, and respond. As listeners, if we accept a mere "receiver" role rather than a "partner in communication" role, we are likely to perceive our only power as the power to tune in or out—the power Jack employs when he doesn't come quickly to his mat for the story.

Our listening goal needs to be more than "absorbing" or we diminish our humanity. We diminish our conceptual abilities. We diminish the co-creation of shared meaning.

Yes, it does take mental effort to listen with energy. To repeat the Hauerwas and Willimon suggestion, "There is no hearing of the word apart from a people who are struggling to listen truthfully to God's word."[4] That's right, "struggling."

Beyond the destructive *attitudes* of passiveness and dependence on the speaker are some destructive listening *behaviors*. Listeners think much faster than speakers can speak. It is nearly impossible to fill our minds with the speaker's words, and the speaker's words only. The words may trigger other thoughts—related or unrelated to the intended meanings. If your mind begins to go beyond the words of the speaker, you are normal. Don't interpret such thought as "daydreaming" or "the speaker is not holding my attention" or "I am not a good listener." Count on extraneous thoughts. You think faster than your preacher preaches.

Your goal as a listener is to discipline those thoughts so that your mental processes are engaged with the content of the sermon—examining, comprehending, evaluating, and appreciating the preachers' words. Such listening takes conscious effort, but is quite possible. As long as you are there for a sermon, why not make the most of it?

You must be motivated to listen. Our lives are generally so full that during a sermon it is easy to let the mind wander to tasks or relationships needing our attention at work and at home. We rarely concentrate on the immediate moment we are living; competent listening requires such concentration.

How do we acquire this necessary motivation? How do we battle complacency? You may be thinking that speakers must provide that motivation, and what a pleasure when they do. But that doesn't always happen, does it? Even if the speaker avoids life application ideas, bypasses inspiration as a goal, or mutters through a manuscript, it is possible for you to make meanings that are valuable.

Often, we simply "get used to" the organizational style and delivery style of our preacher. So used to it, that tuning out becomes easier and easier with each passing week. Sure, you can wish for your preacher to change, but you need to do some changing too. One surveyed listener referenced a preacher who had not made much progress in speech communication competence, but whose insights were worth the listening struggle.

Communication scholars Wolvin and Coakley, authors of the textbook, *Listening*, suggest six listening attitudes essential for motivating the necessary mental effort:[5]

(1) *Interested* (not disinterested): "I will keep listening because there is the potential for valuable meaning."

(2) *Responsible* (not irresponsible): "Communication is a partnership; the preacher and I will mutually create meaning."

(3) *Other-oriented* (not self-centered): "Being inquisitive about the lives and ideas of others leads me to better listening."

*(4)* *Patient* (not impatient): "I know it can take time to develop meanings; I will restrain myself from displaying impatience inappropriately or prematurely."

*(5)* *Equal* (not superior): "Speakers have the right to communicate openly and freely."[6]

*(6)* *Open-minded* (not close-minded): "I am willing to listen, even when I disagree. I restrain defensive thoughts that impede listening, though I thoroughly evaluate meanings. I work to understand the perspectives of others."

For those who intend to keep listening to sermons for the remainder of their lives, such attitudes are highly recommended. Apparently, say the interviewed preachers, some of us listeners are stuck in the parentheses that follow those attitudes that have just been listed. Remember the interviewed preachers' descriptions of "difficult listeners"? Those who are not processing the sermon, not open to change, give comments only when they disagree, have a reactionary mindset, have been wounded by another preacher, and/or have low expectancy.

There are lots of us "difficult" listeners. Preachers are asking us—as long as we are already seated in the sanctuary—to "process" the sermon. They hope we will be open-minded, not tuning out the second we hear something with which we disagree. They know that previous preachers' behaviors affect the way we process their sermons, but they want an opportunity to make meaning with us. They want us to come with the expectancy that valuable meanings are possible.

Do the preachers say, "Listen to my words," expecting the preschool response of quick and total obedience by all listeners? Not too many preachers are living with that kind of delusionary thinking! Remember how most all interviewed preachers responded when asked, "What would your listeners be like if they had put all your sermons into practice?" Almost every preacher laughed. "That will require some imagination," said one. Preachers know the listener will not simply "hear and obey," like a well-programmed computer responding to a keystroke command. As listeners, are we processing messages or are we just "tuning out"?

If sermon meanings are diminished because we listeners choose to tune out, we have ready excuses. To rely on such excuses means that we are holding the preacher entirely responsible, accepting passivity. Listeners in this sermon survey research spoke loudly and clearly about what they want preachers to do: be relevant, know us better, work to connect spiritual insights to our daily lives. Yes, we want them to treat us as partners; so must also accept the responsibilities of that partnership role ourselves.

Remember the outsider in Section One, looking in, asking the millions who regularly participate in sermon communication, "Why do you listen? What are you expecting?" Low expectancy can be tied right to passivity, closed-mindedness, and disinterest. Sure, you may have been conditioned not to expect a particular preacher to hold your attention or offer what you need. The curious on-looker would remind you that you do have the power to leave the church and find a preacher whose style better motivates your listening energy. You could talk to the preacher, though we all know by now that such behavior is rare. You also know you have the power to just tune out. Let's see, if you're 40, that means approximately 35 more years of preaching . . . 35 years x 52 weeks (let's make it 50, we all get sick sometimes) = 1,750 sermons x 20 minutes. You are consciously planning to waste 35,000 minutes of your life? Yikes.

The goal here is not to motivate listeners to leave their churches, but rather to help us all recognize that we need to make the most of sermon time. Even if our preachers are not treating us like partners, we can empower the sermon time by accepting our role as mutual meaning makers. Our changes in communicative behavior will affect the other. That's right. Remember that "function of human communication"? We affect each other. So, how can you affect your preacher with your listening behavior?

"Okay," listeners may be thinking. "What does she want me to do. Sit up? Pay attention? Quit daydreaming?" Those aren't bad suggestions, but your power is not as limited as you may think! Let's explore the mental power available to those who want to listen, those who are looking for potentially useful meanings, those who don't want to waste thousands of minutes.

While definitions of listening abound, most include some version of the following steps: attending, comprehending, remembering, and evaluating.[7] Several definitions include a final listening step: responding.[8]

## Attending

To increase our listening competency, we must first become *attentive*; focusing on the spoken words and nonverbal behaviors of the preacher. Concentrating. As long as you've chosen to attend physically, attend mentally as well. Let go of incessant thoughts. Jot them down if you need to, so you know they'll be waiting for you later. Listen for any meaning that you might be able to create and connect to those intrusive thoughts. For some, the music or liturgy of a service assists with mental readiness for the sermon. For others, great self-discipline is needed and will take massive effort.

Imagine you are in a class and the teacher announces that after the next 20 minutes of lecturing, he will give you an exam on the lecture material. That exam will count for three-fourths of your course grade. Now, you would have to put aside thoughts regarding how to contest this unfair policy, but you could indeed raise your listening energy level so that you maximized your comprehension and memory for the 20-minute session. You could pass that test. No doubt, your listening energy would be higher than had the announcement not been made, if it had just been another day in class.

If we believe the sermon has potential power, then we can motivate ourselves to pay attention. Just as the preachers tell us, "Every sermon cannot be a masterpiece," so we will be quick to add that every "listen" cannot be a "masterpiece" either. Some weeks, some circumstances are too overwhelming. Stress can affect our ability to concentrate. Of course, preachers remind us that those stressful times may be just when we need to listen most.

## Comprehending

After attention has been focused, a comprehension goal must be set. If the goal is "relax" or "absorb," energy levels will be low. But at least "vegging out" is a notch above "tuning out." A fundamental listening goal for every sermon is to try to answer the simple question, "What was the preacher trying to say?" After the service, try to explain the concept to someone else—to evaluate your level of understanding. Can you make them understand?

Before the sermon, give yourself a listening goal; for example,

- "After listening to this sermon, I will be able to state the key thought orally in a way that makes sense to my children (or neighbor, or co-worker, etc)."
- "During the sermon, I will link the key thought to one experience in my life."
- "After this sermon, I will paraphrase one specific piece of content in a comment for the preacher as I shake her hand."
- "After the sermon, I will paraphrase one specific emotion I experienced and the words used to evoke that emotion. I will speak that paraphrase to my preacher."
- "After the sermon, I will find a related Scripture passage to use in meditation sometime this week."
- "During the sermon, I will envision a detailed image that represents the emotions this sermon evokes, including sights, smells, feelings, tastes, and sounds."

These (and other) listening goals serve as "advance organizers" for your thinking.

This technique is one of the ways to compensate for what you perceive to be a preacher's deficit. If the sermon rambles routinely, plan to re-structure the message in a way that works for your patterns of thought. If your preacher almost always uses abstract ideas, use your extra thought time to create concrete supportive evidence that best illustrates the abstract concept for you. Setting a specific listening goal will aid you in getting to the broader goal of *comprehending*.

## Remembering

Even as you are seeking comprehension of the sermon, there is further listening work to be done. Seek to *remember* the message. Use mnemonic devices, visual cueing, and note-taking if necessary. Link the central thought of the sermon to a long-term memory.

Relish details of the memory, implanting the sermon idea. Said one listener: "A sermon on intercessory prayer made me remember and appreciate how my godly grandfather prayed for me when I was a young boy, and how he planted a seed of faith that grew and grew and matured into my salvation when I trusted Jesus. My grandfather didn't get much education, but he loved the Lord." All these years later, the listener remembers the content about intercessory prayer because during the sermon he was able to link the ideas to a long-term memory.

Listen to remember. Said another listener, "Why don't I talk to the preacher about the sermon? I forget most of it before I get back to the door to shake his hand." We may be forgetting because we are not concentrating. Memory devices recommended by listening experts include:[9]

- *Rehearsing*: Repeat the main points mentally as you are hearing them.

- *Constructing mnemonics*: To remember the components of listening, you might construct the phrase "ARE U?" asking "ARE U listening?" Well, yes, if I A (attend), R(recall), E (evaluate) and U (understand).

- *Regrouping material:* A poorly organized sermon can be a major temptation to "tune out." Instead, organize it yourself. If there are too many points, and you can't tell them from the sub-points create your own outline of main points. Instead of thinking, "Ah. She's rambling again, time to tune out," create an order for the tangent and evaluate the logic of the arguments. Regrouping the material enables you to process the content.

- *Note taking:* Another possible memory device is note taking. In some cases, note taking can actually distract us from creating rich meanings. We have to decide if note taking will be a help or hindrance. Perhaps you have decided to keep a sermon notebook or personal spiritual journal; if so, reflective and processing activities can be more valuable than outlining the sermon. For example, draw the image that you envisioned during the sermon. Children draw on church bulletins all the time; take your turn with content-focused doodling. You might jot down your mnemonic device, such as "ARE U listening." Write your listening goal, and its accomplishment such as "I gave the preacher specific feedback as we shook hands. The content paraphrase I spoke to him was . . ." Note a particularly insightful thought and web your reactions to that thought. For example:

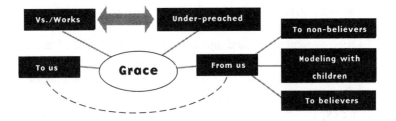

Or maybe you can put the preacher's key idea in your own words, and then brainstorm ways you can apply that idea in the coming week.

If you and your preacher are able to communicate in ways that accomplish those basic listening goals, then remember, as humans, you are capable of even higher levels of thought. We can move on to becoming analytical listeners.

## Evaluating

*Analyze* the message. Use analytical thinking to process the message. Typically, descriptions of analytical thinking include processes like "application, analysis, synthesis, and evaluation."[10] Say critical thinking researchers Paul and Nosich,

> Critical thinking is the intellectually disciplined process of actively and skillfully conceptualizing, applying, analyzing, synthesizing or evaluating information . . . It entails examination of purpose; questions at issues; assumptions; concepts; facts; inferences; implications and consequences; objections from alternative viewpoints; and frame of reference . . .[11]

What does this mean for sermon listeners? In the sermon context, analytical thinking requires: (1) your recognition that your preacher is trying to persuade you, (2) your dissection of the appeals being used, and (3) your conscious choice to be persuaded or not. Really superior preachers will be encouraged by your efforts at analytical thinking. Remember, one of the themes interviewed preachers provided in response to the question, "What do you wish your listeners understood about preaching?" was "Listeners need to think for themselves."

Analytical thinking is a gift you give to yourself and your preacher; it is the antithesis of "tuning out." With tuning out, you don't act on the message because you don't even process the message. With analytical thinking, you may still reject a persuasive attempt, but you do so after co-creating meaning. If your analysis leads you to accept the persuasive attempt, then the results can be transformational.

Analytical listening is not the same as reactionary listening. The reactionary approach has a person listening for ideas with which they automatically disagree, and then either mentally combating for the duration or disconfirming the preacher by tuning out. An analytical listener is . . .

- listening to identify the accuracy of the speaker's claims and the logic of the conclusions being drawn from those claims.[12]
- evaluating the inferences and supportive evidence.
- becoming aware of the emotions the sermon stirs.
- processing speaker integrity related to the topic.
- listening for patterns of faulty reasoning such as:[13]
  *Proposing a false dilemma.* "We must either accept abortion as moral or spend our resources making it illegal again."
  *Jumping to conclusions.* "This humanistic agnostic is not concerned with moral issues; none of them are."
  *Supportive evidence offered without source credibility.* "I read somewhere that single parent mothers cannot discipline as effectively as fathers."
  *Arguing that something is correct because that's the way it has always been done.* "Women and men have had separate Bible study groups since this church began; now some are

suggesting that we've been wrong?"

*Reasoning in a circular pattern.* "No Christian person would ever commit suicide, because suicide is not Christian."

*Attacking the person rather than the issue.* "We cannot accept this approach to studying the Old Testament; look who is suggesting it—a preacher we all know to be a dogmatic, fundamentalist conservative."

*Promoting a "slippery slope."* "If school prayer remains outlawed, then those who pray anywhere will be considered criminals."

*Arguing a cause-effect link, without consideration of other variables.* "The Internet is a new entity in our culture; and the crimes of children are becoming more violent. This violence is the result of the Internet."

Remember, many speakers use faulty reasoning without awareness. If a preacher believes a claim very strongly, that conviction can diminish her own analytical thinking. We need to become acutely conscious of the reasoning used to support "Christian" claims. Certainly, every sermon doesn't need to be an exercise in apologetics, but sloppy use of our mental powers is irresponsible and damaging to the Christian message.

Listeners, if a causal relationship is implied where none has been demonstrated, think it over, but don't assume your preacher is consciously unethical. Ask the preacher about the statement if it troubles you. For example, "You stated that the Internet is the cause of increases in violent crimes; do you leave room for any other variables like mental illness (or drug use, accessibility to weaponry, neglect and abuse, media influence, or cultural desensitization to violence)?" If the preacher defends the fallacious reasoning, you have learned something that affects how you process this persuasive attempt. If the preacher acknowledges that in her zeal to awaken parents to the dangers of the Internet she may have overstated the case, then you have more information to help you form meanings. If a questionable piece of evidence is used and no source cited, ask the preacher for the source so you can check it out.

If listeners don't inquire about the reasoning preachers use in their sermons, some preachers will inadvertently continue to use their pulpit authority to promote claims with faulty reasoning. If listeners are lazy about analytical thinking, they do a disservice to the mutual mental growth of their preachers and themselves. Consequently, people may keep making observations such as Mark Noll's in *The Scandal of the Evangelical Mind*: "Notwithstanding all their other virtues, however, American evangelicals are not exemplary for their thinking, and they have not been so for several generations." Christian preachers and listeners who are not evangelical, don't be too quick to distinguish yourself from the stinging accusation. We all need to hold ourselves and each other accountable for using sound reasoning. Especially in the church.[14]

Of course, spiritual matters are not limited to research reports and linear argument. But neither should we embrace careless reasoning or glib generalities when we make spiritual conclusions. For example, a few folks heard something like this from a pulpit: "I heard Dr. Laura talking about some Internet site where they said rapists don't really hurt anybody. I suppose now it won't be a crime anymore. Has everybody in this country gone mad?"

Analytical listeners will demand that questions be asked, like, "Who said it?" "What did they say?" "On what did they base their opinion?" "Do you know that in the name of 'free speech' anyone can say anything on the Internet?" "Does anyone other than the person who said it agree with the statement?" "Is there any evidence that anyone has agreed with it?" "Has any state government even considered a proposal to have the illegal status of rape removed?" The statement paraphrasing Dr. Laura is indeed disturbing, but cited without contextual information, some may be quick to reach conclusions that are not particularly logical. The statement fits our Christian preconceptions about the demoralization of this country, and so we may just accept the fallacious "slippery slope" reasoning. A listener could easily "interpret" this preacher's statement, repeating it as, "Some research said rape isn't really bad and now they are trying to make it legal. The preacher said so." Unfortunately, this scenario is not fictitious. This kind of inadequate thinking is altogether too common in the church.

Analytical thinking is central to high levels of communication

competency. Of course, many, many preachers are exemplary thinkers. Following their argument paths can be a listening treat. With
such preachers, we can learn analytical thinking skills by listening
to their tightly reasoned arguments woven into contemporary narratives. To ask listeners and preachers to be aware of their reasoning is not an insult, but a call for collaboration. A call to continue
to grow our internal language processes as we co-create meanings
via the external spoken word. From mind—through mouth—to
mind.

Of course, poor speaking habits can be difficult to ignore. Some
are minor and irritating, "like, you know, vocal, um, fillers." (I
once counted 67 uses of the word "essentially" in a 60-minute
lecture.) Other habitual problems may be moderately challenging
like the tangent that comes as regular as clockwork in an otherwise adequate presentation. And still other incompetencies are
exceptionally frustrating to the listener, influencing the meaning
being created; for example, gender bias, a contentious or negative
tone, too much information with no oral organizational cues, fallacious reasoning, no scriptural link, or a continual display of ignorance regarding listeners' lives.

Discipline yourself to filter out the minor distracting mannerisms. Some listeners actually close their eyes to concentrate more
fully, though the preacher will not appreciate such a response. When
a moderate problem like a "red flag" phrase is spoken (a phrase
that raises your defenses), remind yourself that you and your
preacher disagree about a particular concept; don't get de-railed
for the rest of the sermon. Many of us "rehearse our response" to
words with which we disagree, and then miss what else is being
said.[15]

If you obsess on the objectionable phrase, you may start focusing on everything you dislike about the sermon, the preacher, previous sermons, and the church. Instead, set the phrase aside
mentally. Respect that your preacher may have something else to
offer. Work to build a trusting relationship that allows you to talk
to the preacher about that issue. You and your preacher will not
agree about every matter. Accept it. Do you agree about *everything* with any other human being? Controversial issues are at the

heart of preaching; the goal is a persuasive goal—so of course you won't agree with everything.

Quibbling regarding non-central issues is non-productive. Engaging in meaningful dialogue regarding complex spiritual issues can be enlightening, mentally stimulating, and worthwhile. There is a big difference between the dialogue and the quibble. As sermon listeners, we want our preachers to know when we disagree, when we spot faulty logic, when we are derailed by red flag words, or lost in the rambling. But, apparently, we don't tell them. Why not? Maybe the kind of relationship necessary for dialogue has not been established. Maybe the role of preacher as "God's Messenger" inhibits our responses. Maybe we feel powerless, and assume that the preacher thinks we are agreeing with everything because we are in the listening role. Whatever the reason for our silence and the possible resentment and reactionary listening behaviors that flow from perceptions of low-power, we must work to change the nature of our relationships with our preachers. That is, if we believe the sermon has the possibility of positive effect.

If you are fortunate enough to have a preacher whose sermons are usually well organized, inspirational, clear, insightful, conversational, relevant, Scripture-based, and life-application driven, don't become complacent. Work to mentally paraphrase the preacher's words. Make conscious decisions regarding the preacher's persuasive efforts. Keep your verbal and nonverbal feedback during the sermon alive and discernible. Follow through when you accept a call to action. Encourage your preacher to "keep it up" with specific content-related feedback. If the preacher trains you to expect such high quality sermons and then has an "off" week, work harder at your listening. Never assume the preacher has "arrived." Ask your preacher if the church system functions so he has adequate preparation time, continual listener input, time away for retreat and refreshment, and access to other preachers for dialogue and fresh ideas. You may need to write a letter to the church leadership requesting that such needs be addressed. Enable the preacher to keep sermon preparation as a high priority. Welcome attempts at creativity. If your preacher's sermons are highly competent and your listening energy is high as well, your opportunities for individual, family, church, community, and cultural transformation are tremendous.

Listeners, your listening behavior is an indispensable component of the preaching partnership. Your choices regarding listening energy levels can dramatically increase or decrease the power of the spoken word during the sermon. Now can you see that the responsibility for making meaning does not rest entirely in the pulpit? Listeners, I am urging you to embrace your role as partners in sermon communication.

As you know by now, *The Great American Sermon Survey* emanates from a communication perspective. This perspective promotes the listener as an active participant in the mutual endeavor of meaning creation. That's why so much of what is written here is based on what surveyed listeners have to say about their preachers. In this sermon survey research, your perspective is validated as real and important. As sermon listeners it feels pretty good to have preachers *listen* to our voices, doesn't it? But don't "Amen" before recognizing that the promotion of partnership preaching is a message directed at all who communicate during sermon time. Are you up for it? Listening improves with practice, say the experts.[16] Each sermon gives you another opportunity to practice.

Do you actually believe sermons can be a powerful, positive part of your life? Then listen. Listen to your preacher's words.

For further suggestions to help you maximize the power of your role in the sermon communication partnership, keep reading.

## Notes

[1] Verdeber, R. (1987). *Communicate!* (5th ed.). Belmont, CA: Wadsworth Publishing, 92.

[2] Pinker, S. (1994). *The language instinct.* New York: William Morrow, 227.

[3] Higbee, K. (1988). *Your memory: How it works and how to improve it* (2nd ed.). Englewood Cliffs, NJ: Prentice Hall.

[4] Hauerwas, S., & Willimon, W.H. (1990). *Resident aliens: Life in the Christian colony.* Nashville, TN: Abingdon Press, 128.

[5] Wolvin, A., & Coakley, C.G. (1996). *Listening.* Boston, MS: McGraw-Hill, 135–136.

[6] See Wolvin, & Coakley, 137.

[7] See Wolvin, & Coakley, 70–71.

[8] See Verderber, R. (1996). *Communicate!* (8th ed.). Belmont, CA: Wadsworth Publishing, 140.

[9] See Verderber, 1996, 148.

[10] Halpern, D.E. (1992). "A national assessment of critical thinking skills in adults: Taking steps toward the goal." Paper submitted to the National Center for Education Statistics. Washington, D.C.

[11] Paul, R., & Nosich, G.M. (1991). "A proposal for the national assessment of higher-order thinking." Paper submitted to the national Center for Educational Statistics, Washington, D.C, 4–5.

[12] Kearney, P., & Plax, T.G. (1996). *Public speaking in a diverse society.* Mountain View, CA: Mayfield Publishing, 141.

[13] Described in many persuasion texts and public speaking texts. e.g., Schick, T., & Jr., Vaughn, L. (1995). *How to think about weird things: Critical thinking for a new age.* Mountain View, CA: Mayfield.; Sprague, J., & Stuart, D. (1996). *The speaker's handbook.* Orlando, FL: Harcourt Brace Company; and Woodward, G.C., & Denton, R.E. Jr. (1996). *Persuasion and influence in American life* (3rd ed.). Prospect Heights, IL: Waveland Press.

[14] Noll, M.A. (1994). *The scandal of the evangelical mind.* Grand Rapids, MI: William B. Eerdmans Publishing Company, 3.

[15] See Verderber, 1987.

[16] Higbee, K.L.(1988). *Your memory: How it works and how to improve it* (2nd ed.). Englewood Cliffs, NJ: Prentice Hall.

Chapter 9

# Listening to the Listeners

**A**N ADVERTISEMENT in *Preaching* magazine announces an upcoming preacher's conference "specifically tailored to you and your ministry" with "inspirational messages, practical workshops, spiritual enrichment, and speakers who understand you and your life."[1] It sounds as though when preachers step into the role of listener, they want what their own listeners want; public face-to-face human communication with relevancy, inspiration, life application, insight, and content connected to their lives!

Stepping into the "listening" role can be educational for preachers. Said one interviewed preacher, "I don't hear very many preachers that I like. Most of them preach sermons that are trite and not very well organized." A few Sundays in a pew can assist the preacher in gaining the listener's perspective. But beyond such attempts to "switch roles" for a little enlightenment is a fundamental principle of human interaction: *We are all listeners.*

A listener disagrees. When she reflects upon her attempts to engage the preacher in dialogue, she concludes that it is "impossible" because "He is not a listener. He's a teller." If the transformation you hope for is ever to materialize, preacher, you must listen intently to your listeners. Preachers, you have two texts: Scripture and your people.

*The Great American Sermon Survey* revealed that most of you preachers spend most of your sermon preparation time and effort studying the scriptural text. Nothing in this book suggests that you should diminish those efforts. Nearly everything in this book suggests that your efforts to study the "text" of your listeners do need to increase. Don't create a false dichotomy—spiritual truth versus listeners. Study both. You have two texts.

Preachers, do you know the listeners' ideas and feelings on your next sermon topic or text? Could you state them to the listeners' satisfaction as you begin to prepare your sermon? Some formal mechanism for collecting listeners' perceptions must be established. **Preachers can invigorate their sermons with creativity, novelty, and relevancy, by actively pursuing the listeners' perspectives and integrating those perspectives into each and every sermon.**

Preachers, your listeners' lives are your greatest resource. If this book leads you to make one and only one change, please, create a formal process by which to gather listeners' input for upcoming sermons. Announce topics and texts well in advance, provide a "Sermon Support" box in a conspicuous location, and invite listeners to contribute their "ideas, comments, and questions."

Form a group of listeners with whom to dialogue about upcoming sermons. If a threatening climate exists, then hand-selected "supporters" can comprise your first listener support group as you ease yourself into the partnership mode and as you ease listeners into the process of authentic dialogue. You may also wish to hold open-invitation breakfasts, brown-bag lunches, or evening dessert sermon chats, so you can listen to your listeners talk about approaching sermon content.

Initially, you may need to formulate some open-ended questions to promote the discussion, but as much as possible, be a listener, not a dialogue director, as you gather listeners to talk about your upcoming content. As preacher, you will need to demonstrate your openness to the thoughts of others, replacing judgmental responses with probing questions that promote elaboration. As a climate of trust develops, a free-flowing discussion with preacher as "eavesdropper" may ensue. Eventually, the preacher might even consult the group on *process*, directing the discussion by saying, "I'm thinking about trying a case study method on the story of Joseph. Here's the process idea . . . How would you respond as a listener?" But in general, the dialogue should focus on content more than process.

In a large church, a rotational system of selecting listeners by demographics (ages of life, stages of life, gender, culture/ethnicity/race, work type, etc.) may be needed. Groups of less than ten are desirable, though larger groups can be broken into smaller sections and asked to report back to the whole. Preachers in large churches with groups already in place (such as "cell groups" or "Bible study" groups) could ask the group leaders to devote some group time each month to discussion of upcoming sermon topics. Group leaders could then forward a summary of the ideas or a relevant story from someone's life. E-mail "Sermon Support" discussion is a great method for encouraging participation from those with access to technology who just can't make time for a face-to-face meeting. Establishing a church web site with a sermon chat room is an idea whose time may have come! (Just be sure other avenues, such as the "Sermon Support" box, are available for those without access to computers.)

## Sermon Support Group Guidelines

*Be as open as possible in your invitations, so no one is excluded.* If your hostile climate has led you to select "supporters" for your first group discussion, don't let that practice continue indefinitely. If the church is small enough, have an open invitation. If not, be sure the invitation process is systematic, so that everyone is eventually invited to contribute.

*Provide a "Sermon Support" box form,* with a space for the contributor's name (so you can contact the contributing listener if necessary), but allow for anonymity by writing "optional" under the space for the name. A listener reluctant to be a partner in sermon communication needs a safe way to get started. You can include sentence starters on the form, such as "I've often wondered about . . ." or "Thinking about this topic reminds me of the time when . . ." Be sure listeners know they can drop relevant articles, cartoons, and other printed materials into the "Sermon Support" box as well.

*Actually use the material you gather!* There is no quicker way to kill this idea than to ignore everything you hear from listeners because it doesn't fit with your predetermined plan.

*Be careful of confidentiality.* Listeners should be made aware that their contributions to such a dialogue might be used in the sermon. If a discussion leads to a spontaneous self-disclosure that is emotional or potentially embarrassing, be sure to check with the listener about whether or not she wants you to use the story. You can build fictional narratives based on various listener experiences, ensuring a realistic and relevant illustration. In general, seek a narrative that reveals "what I learned through an experience" or "how I came to understand" rather than "what I did wrong."

*When your listeners are sharing ideas, listen.* Take notes. Reflect. Whether you find a perfect illustration from a listener's life or your thoughts are simply catapulted in a direction they hadn't gone before, the discussion allows you to better connect to listeners because you "know where they are coming from" on your sermon topic. Can you paraphrase your listeners' perspectives to their satisfaction before you begin sermon preparation? If so, the insistently ringing call for relevancy will be answered!

*Work at least six weeks ahead* so that you are collecting listener ideas in advance of your private preparation time. Writing your outline or manuscript in advance of the dialogue will minimize the impact of the process as you try to just "stick in" an isolated idea from a listener. Rather, let their conversation initiate your preparation, let their comments serve as springboard for your insight, organizational pattern, etc.

Preachers, if the sermon support group becomes an integral part of your sermon preparation, not only will the transformational power of the spoken words of your sermons be enhanced, but the church community will be strengthened through the resulting relationships.

Now, listeners, how can you become "sermon supporters"? You can begin by implementing several of the following suggestions, accepting your responsibility as a partner in the preaching process. You could also promote the partnership approach among other listeners. Discuss this book together. The group could then work as a team to accomplish as many of the following suggestions as possible.

### Before the sermon

- Request topics/texts ahead of time. Perhaps they can be printed on a church calendar or newsletter.
- Read the text prior to the sermon. Think about the topic.
- Get ready to listen physically and mentally.
- Suggest the "Sermon Support" box idea to your preacher. Write a comment or question on a regular basis.
- If your preacher has a sermon support group, be sure to participate as much as possible. If you are invited to attend a sermon support dialogue, attend if at all possible. If you can't be present, be accountable to the preacher with some written input and a brief explanation since the preacher will likely interpret non-attendance or no response as "no interest."
- Share this book with your preacher.
- Share sermon ideas, comments, questions, or related printed material with the preacher.
- Respect preparation time. Perhaps you will need to organize a "pastoral care" group, with rotating membership. This group can assist the preacher in meeting the practical and emotional needs of the church community.
- Ask the preacher if the church system is structured to provide enough preparation time; seek to change the system if necessary.
- Begin to use a Sermon Notebook or journal which you bring with you to the sermons.
- Be conscious of your own expectations (Inspiration? Comfort? Life application?). Listen for what you need but be aware of other possibilities as well.
- Start a rotational sermon support prayer group or designate a time each week that listeners will pray for the preacher as she or he prepares the sermon.

## During

- Sit toward the front if those seats are usually empty.
- Display a high degree of attentiveness with whatever verbal and nonverbal behaviors are appropriate in your church tradition or cultural background.
- Set a listening goal. Don't listen to "grade" or "score" the preacher's "performance" in the partnership. (You could, however, grade *yourself* based on the accomplishment of your listening goal.)
- Listen to create meaning. Be mindful of the potential for valuable, positive transformation.
- Use the suggestions regarding attention, comprehension, memory, and analytical thinking delineated in the previous chapter.

## After

- Reflect on the meaning you and your preacher have co-created.
- Plan a comment for your preacher. Be sure it is focused on content whenever possible. Avoid post-sermon evaluative remarks like "good" or "confusing" or the intended neutral, interpreted negatively, "Have a nice day," that doesn't even acknowledge that sermon communication has just occurred. An easy and appreciated technique? Paraphrase the key point, speak the one-sentence content or feeling paraphrase to your preacher, and then ask the preacher if you are on target.
- If you can't speak to the preacher, speak to someone else in the church community about the meaning of the sermon. Again, not a conversation to score the preacher, but a conversation related to the way the communication has affected you.

- Organize a note-writing campaign so the preacher receives several notes each week with expanded content-based comments. (Use e-mail if you and the preacher are on-line.) This idea is especially important for churches in which everyone doesn't have the opportunity to give the preacher a verbal comment. Remember, the interviewed preachers wanted you to know: "Preachers would preach themselves to death if someone encouraged them a little." "Encouragement" doesn't equal "compliment"; knowing that people are actually thinking about what they say would be more "encouraging" to preachers than listeners may be able to imagine. Remember the interviewed preacher who said that if he asks for feedback he's afraid "they might think I'm 'insecure' or 'fishing for compliments'"? The goal is not to provide preachers with continuous compliments, but to engage our thoughts, and the preacher's thoughts, in the continuing creation of meaning, to focus on the way sermon communication "affects us." For many preachers, it would be a radical, heart-warming, spirit invigorating, revolutionary change to start receiving content-based sermon reflections from their listeners on a regular basis.

Examples of "at the door," "e-mail" or "note" sermon follow-ups from listeners:
- "That last point made me start to wonder how we can be servants to each other in the church."
- "I've been working to improve my memory. Did I get your six main points down right?"
- "When you described your grandfather's farm, I could almost smell the hay."
- "I honestly never understood before how the books of the Bible were selected. Thanks. Could you suggest any reading material on the subject?"
- "That doctrine has been a mystery to me. You really spoke with clarity. Thank you."

- "You motivated me to 'live the beatitudes,' but I don't know where to start. Do I just try to be meeker, or do I work on my spiritual journey and wait for meekness to come?"
- "Your last sentence was worded so well, I'm sure I will remember it for a long time."
- "I had never even noticed that word 'look' in that verse about Moses and the burning bush before. I will be 'looking' for spiritual messages this week. I'll let you know what I find."
- "With my boss, 'nice' behavior is seen as 'sucking up.' It makes him suspicious. I'm going to be thinking about practical ways to love him with the *agape* love principles you described; it just doesn't seem possible."

These kinds of substantive comments contribute to a trusting climate among sermon communication partners. When such a climate exists and you have demonstrated your "tuned-in" listening, then you and your preacher may be ready for private dialogue about an issue that is "major" to you. Requesting private time with the preacher to discuss a concern is difficult; if such a "discussion" is the first you've ever had with the preacher about a sermon, then the difficulty is magnified. Plan a way to begin the conversation, plan to listen to the responses before you react, and plan for interaction, not "saying my piece" to the priest or "getting it off my chest." Plan the first words you will say.

"I've noticed that you seem to feel it's important for us to agree with your creationism perspective," or "I feel left out when you choose illustrations that are based almost exclusively in male experiences."

Listeners, let's consider some general guidelines for discussing difficult issues with your preacher:

- Speak for yourself, don't say "we" or "lots of people" unless you are representing a group of people who are willing to be identified by name.
- Speak in private, face-to-face. Such dialogue should not take place on e-mail.
- Reserve such dialogue for the major issues.

- Be concise and specific.
- Explain your perception and how it was derived.
- Identify and claim your emotional reaction (frustrated, angry, confused, etc.)
- Don't exaggerate to make your point. ("I am really very irate!" when actually "I feel irritated" is more realistic.)
- Be ready to share specific examples of your general comment.
- Be ready to repeat your perspective; in a defensive climate you may need to rephrase your thoughts as many as three times before you are "heard."
- Be sure your voice reflects your partnership attitude.
- Don't threaten. "If you don't listen [connotation "obey"] then I'm leaving this church [or going to the board, or whatever]."
- Expect a meaningful dialogue rather than a time for you to scold or be scolded.
- Actually listen to the responses of the preacher.
- Have an empathic listening goal: to understand the preacher's perspective on this issue. Try to rephrase the preacher's response so you are both aware that meaning is shared. ("So you believe your views of creationism are central to the Christian experience and you repeat them frequently because you know there are people in the parish who hold a different belief?" "So since you don't consciously intend to demonstrate a male bias, you believe that I should overlook your language choices?")
- Metacommunicate—talk about the situation. ("I know this is uncomfortable; I feel awkward approaching you, but the issue is important to me; I want to share my viewpoint—do you want to hear it?" "I feel frustrated that you do not understand what I'm trying to say. Let me explain it once more and then you could try to paraphrase what you think I'm saying.")
- Suggest solutions if appropriate. ("I am wishing for sermons that are more connected to my daily life. Since you preach at three small churches every Sunday, we don't get to talk with you before or after the sermon. It must be hard for you to get to know us. Could I help you conduct a survey of the

listeners? You could use the specific information about our families, work, and spiritual journeys to personalize your sermons.")

Listener, even if you are the only one in your church who implements these suggestions, you will discover your power to affect the preacher and the sermon. If you've read this far, the phrase "mutual responsibility for co-creating meaning" has become familiar. Now, take it to heart. Activate that familiar phrase as you seek to be a more competent communicator during sermon interaction.

What else can preachers do to listen to their listeners? As an occasional clarity check-up, why not provide a small sheet of paper in each bulletin, with the following instructions written on the top: *Following today's sermon, please write the key idea of the sermon in your own words. Drop this one sentence paraphrase into the "Sermon Support" box on your way out the door. Thank you.* As you read the responses, your question as preacher then becomes, "Am I satisfied that they understood? Did we co-create meaning?" Remember not to ask, "Did you like it?" but rather "What meanings did you create as you listened?"

Once a student approached me wanting to present a speech on her life's passion, classical music. I asked her how she thought her classmate audience might react. "I don't think most of them like classical," she responded. (What an understatement!) She asked for a show of hands—not one classmate shared her interest. Then she asked everyone to jot down the style of music they *did* like and to name their favorite song. She used that information to "decenter" her speech to her apathetic audience. Using tapes and various instruments, she connected segments of classical music to movie theme songs and every style of music her classmates liked. Her goal was accomplished—students became more informed about classical music; they even stopped rolling their eyes at each other. When no one showed interest, this novice but wise speaker did not discard the topic (her belief in the beauty and value of classical music), she just approached it from the listeners' perspective rather than her own. She *decentered* the speech.

Decentering is the process of moving away from perceiving yourself as the center and moving toward presenting the sermon, as much as possible, from a perspective that resonates with the listeners. Dance and Zak-Dance explain decentering:

> A speech, much like a piece of clothing that has been tailored to the knowledge, interests, attitudes, and expectations of the audience; that answers potential questions; that clears up ambiguities . . . is going to "fit" the audience better than a speech "off the rack." [Such a speech has a] far greater chance of accomplishing the speaker's specific purpose.[2]

Olford suggests that "relevance" is so familiar a mandate to preachers that it has become jargon. Preachers need to plan specific action to assure relevance, not assume it. In *The Speaker's Handbook*, authors Sprague and Stuart proclaim, "Audience analysis . . . is much more than a step in planning your speech. It is the constant awareness of those who are the 'co-authors' of your speech."[3] Sometimes speakers are oblivious to the minds of the audience: "Here is how I see this issue. You should see it the same way."

Sometimes speakers make stereotypical assumptions about their listeners. One of my students told about a previous professor who chastised students with comments like, "You college students don't know what it's like to be politically active. I've never seen one protest on this campus." As a volunteer involved in a wide array of work with various community groups, the student was very offended. She explained to me, "How can he assume I don't care about the political issues of my community? He's certainly never seen my resumé." Likewise, a preacher may assume, "Mostly older people here. They'll never want to change." Or, "I'll just change the punch line from 'accountant' to 'factory worker' since there are lots of blue-collar folks here."

Such assumptive thinking is not the same as decentering. Decentering answers the pivotal listener's question: "How does this content resonate with what is already meaningful to us?"

Decentering can only be accomplished when the speaker has a thorough understanding of the listeners' perspectives. Decentering is necessary for communication competence.

In one way, this decentering process and the whole notion of the preaching partnership may not be palatable to preachers who have been taught to "keep a careful distance from my people." Keeping relationships *appropriate* is absolutely necessary for preachers. But such a concern is not a valid excuse for not keeping relationships at all. Be careful about self-disclosure with some of your listeners? Yes, some are not ready for deep authenticity. Everyone cannot be your best friend. But that is not a defense for living a life of pretense, especially since trust develops as a reciprocal response to self-disclosure. And yes, you bring spiritual messages to the listeners, you are a leader. But that role does not automatically set you so far apart from your listeners that you can no longer hear their voices. Decentering? The *exegesis* of your listeners![4] Says Lenore Tisdale,

> Good preaching requires its practitioners to become adept in "exegeting" local congregations and their contexts, so they can proclaim the gospel in relevant and transformative ways for particular communities of faith.[5]

Remember immediacy, remember relevancy, remember connection? Then pursue decentering. Specific decentering techniques include:[6]

- Seek information about your listeners, as a group and as individuals.
- Observe your listeners at church and community functions with the explicit goal of understanding faith through their eyes.
- Gather the collective history of the church. Compile stories; interview individuals from various demographic groups; examine archival materials for chronology and theme; predict a demographic profile, then create an actual demographic profile—examine your assumptions by contrasting the two profiles; catalogue rituals; chronicle events and activities.

Group experience creates collectives of meaning that the preacher must understand. A sense of current community is predicated upon collective history.

- Seek to use convergent language rather than divergent language. Use language that brings you together as community, rather than language that distinguishes preacher from listeners and calls attention to differences. The goal is to increase *shared* meaning.

- Conduct systematic data collection as suggested in previous chapters. Avoid questions like "What do you think of my preaching?" The goal is understanding your listeners' lives and spiritual journeys. Use open-ended questions. Plan your data collection carefully so listeners take the process seriously. Share the results. Use the results.

- Create informal and formal dialogue sessions or focus groups. Establish these processes as integral, ongoing components of sermon preparation.

- Seek an informant, a contact person who has a history with the church. Ask questions. Listen.

- Make intelligent inferences. Then check your perceptions. ("It seems like people look away when I mention changing the communion process. Is this a sensitive issue?")

- Work toward empathy with every listener. Even when the life circumstance or attitude of a listener is far removed from any you have experienced, ask yourself, "When have I felt a similar feeling?"

- "Job shadow" your listeners. Discern listeners or listener groups whose life experiences are quite different from your own. With permission, of course, "job shadow" listeners for a morning to better understand their daily context. Take them to lunch and talk about the experience. Ask, "How does your Christian faith intersect with your workplace? What kinds of sermons do you need to enable your spiritual growth?"

- Take a class in ethnography and use your listeners as a project. Read the invaluable book, *Preaching as Local Theology and Folk Art,* by Lenore Tubbs Tisdale.[7]

- Conceive of your listeners as a separate co-culture, tracking areas where a lack of shared meaning (with the preacher perspective) exists. Notice language usage differences. Keep a running "preacher-jargon" list. Check it with listeners by asking if you ever use those words.

- Use analogy. Says Stephen Farris, author of *Preaching that Matters*, "We need, then, in our preaching a way of linking the world of the biblical text and the world in which we live and preach that affirms similarity but respects dissimilarity. Analogy can be the link between worlds that we need."[8]

- Accept the diversity of your listener group as real and potentially beneficial. As many preachers have noted, listeners approach sermon time from multiple vantage points: age, gender, belief or non-belief, degree of commitment to their faith, co-culture, race, ethnicity, church background, socioeconomic status, and position/action on each sermon topic. Using language that brings people together as a "community" while simultaneously acknowledging, respecting, and decentering to their various vantage points is no small challenge. But it is a common challenge. Knowing your listeners is the difficult solution to addressing differences. The listener themes that emerge from this sermon survey research can be incredibly helpful to preachers wondering what unites their listeners. Analyzing your specific listener group will be even more helpful.

## A Sermon Communication Style Suited for Listening

Sermon delivery styles vary. This statement surprises no one. Preachers have different communication styles which have developed over time. Usually preachers feel comfortable with their style. Most use a phrase outline or an outline with some manuscripting. When listeners reference delivery, they are adamantly against being read to in a monotone voice. They want warmth, passion, and a conversational manner. And at the heart of many of the listeners' complaints about organizational problems may be the preachers' dependence on a literary style for an oral process.

While some preachers are able to construct and deliver sermons in an oral style, interpreting their manuscript with vocal expression that enhances meaning, many others write in a literary style and then wonder why listeners don't appreciate their efforts. At the heart of excellent sermon delivery is a complete immersion—not a sprinkling—a complete immersion in the power of the *spoken* word.

Preachers need to develop an oral style, use oral rehearsal, attune themselves to the artistry of spoken language, and understand that the voice is their primary instrument. Orality is the key to powerful preaching. If you want to learn an "ideal number" of gestures to insert in every sermon, you'll need to look elsewhere. If you believe in the potential power and dynamism of the spoken word, read on.

Based on Walter Ong's writings, Frank Dance and Carol Zak-Dance conclude, "Oral and written styles differ. Whereas a written style is best suited for reading, an oral style is best suited to listening. What makes a good novel is not what makes a good speech."[9] A sermon suited for listening. *Listening.*

If you doubt this contrast, try reading aloud from a medical journal or a VCR manual. To put it mildly, such literary forms do not lend themselves best to being heard in acoustic space. Logical, rational? Yes. Written to be heard? No. Poetry exemplifies the oral noetic; meant for a "listen," not for a "read"—alliteration, rhyme, and onomatopoeia find their best expression with the *spoken* word.

The sermon is an oral event and needs to be crafted with an oral style, oral preparation, and an "ear" for oral artistry. An oral noetic, or oral way of knowing, is the basis for the most powerful speeches. Indeed, an oral noetic includes aiding the listener's auditory memory with redundancy and word choice, alluding to common life experiences and connections between speaker and audience, and revealing emotion through the voice.[10]

When Dance and Zak-Dance contrast the oral noetic with a literary noetic, they explain that the oral noetic includes "short and simple words, short and simple sentences, more use of questions, more personal pronouns, more contractions, more use of colloquial expressions, frequent use of transitions, repetition, internal summaries, and more direct adaptation to the immediate audience."[11] In addition, they tell us, "Spoken materials, unlike written works, should be prepared for a well-defined and specified audience, spoken language must be readily understood . . . Spoken language, through feedback, can be quickly adapted to the situation."[12]

An oral style is not an inferior logic, but a different logic. It does not insult our literate minds, but rather speaks to our listening ears, acknowledging the reality of the oral-aural process. For example, the "flashback" can work well with a visual medium, but could become quite confusing in a speech. Literature written in an oral style is often called "thought provoking" and "enjoyable" (Shel Silverstein's *The Giving Tree*) or "inspiring" and "engaging" (Max Lucado's *The Great House of God*). Lucado introduces one chapter in that book with these sentences:

> I'd like you to think about someone. His name is not important. His looks are immaterial. His gender is of no concern. His title is irrelevant. He is important not because of who he is, but because of what he did. He went to Jesus on behalf of a friend.[13]

Now if I were grading those sentences as part of a student research paper, I would write "REVISE" on the top, noting the fragments and repetitive sentence structure. But when I "hear" the words, allowing myself to read with an ear for the oral noetic, I give a grade of "excellent."

If you've read either work, you know that those pieces of literature are not limited in purpose to inspiration or joy; the works are persuasive and rich in insight, and the oral style opens our minds to the possibilities of change. Oral style does not depend on direct explanations. For another example of "oral style" re-read the concluding words in Section One of this book. I could have just said, "There are phrases such as 'Will you marry me?' that can change the people who hear and speak them." But I didn't. I chose an oral style to illustrate the *concept* I was proposing: *The spoken word is powerful.*

An oral style requires orality in preparation. Say many surveyed preachers, "My fear is that it won't all come together during the sermon." That particular fear can be eradicated with oral rehearsal as the sermon comes together before the appointed hour.

As portions of outline or manuscript are drafted, they need to be "tried out" orally, tested for their spoken power. Rearranged. Regrouped. Revised. As each section of the sermon is developed, the preacher needs to converse his or her way through the logic. An oral product begs for oral preparation. Oral rehearsal allows for prediction of length; mental rehearsal does not. Of all the preparation strategies public speakers employ, my colleague Kent Menzel and I found that oral rehearsal for an audience is the preparation strategy most predictive of public speaking excellence.[14]

As listeners in this study request relevancy and a voice that displays emotion and relationship with the listener, as listeners ask that monotone reading and jargon use be relinquished, as they wish for preachers who "speak with us, not at us," they are requesting an oral noetic, an oral style.

This oral style is the basis for the power of the spoken word, the power of the spoken sermon. If we abdicate that power, relying on a "literary" approach, the sermon may indeed diminish in power until it becomes an invisible presence in the culture. While the media can exploit the visual modality, and technology can expand the size of the audience, the face-to-face sermon gains its power as it capitalizes on its strength—its spoken nature. A monologic, literary style sermon fails to employ its latent endowments. Most books do not converse with you; a sermon can and should be structured as a conversation. The mental participation of the listeners is predicated on the oral style.

That vocal "passion" listeners want can come with the oral style. Say some preachers, "I'm not dynamic. It's just not my personality." But the spoken word itself is dynamic and your attention to the use of your voice can expand the power of your sermon exponentially. Do you embody the words? If you are thinking ahead to your next point, thinking back to a stuttered word, berating yourself for not preparing more thoroughly, or processing anger toward the sleeping man on the front row, you will not embody your words. Your voice is the pivotal tool of your sermon delivery. Plan pauses, emphases, rate changes, vocal variation, whispers, and more—to engage the listeners in co-creating meaning. Demonstrate the emotion of the text, the relationship God wants with the listeners, the sacredness of the moment, the vitality of the application, the encouragement, the comfort, the strength of the sermon—with your voice.

Pursuing an oral noetic is a change that would lead many preachers to a more powerful use of the spoken word in their sermons as well as a more powerful partnership with their listeners. An oral product needs an oral preparation process. Rehearse orally, tune in to the sounds of the voice, and contemplate language choices carefully. You are communicating more than artistry; the oral noetic is a central component of your message.

Preachers, in this chapter you've been implored to *listen to your listeners*. Have you heard what the surveyed listeners are saying? They want inspiration, life application, insight, and information presented in relevant ways, with clear ties to Scripture, organized for auditory processing, and delivered conversationally. Such a sermon is the challenge. Such a sermon can reach all types of listeners. Such a sermon can be transformative. Such a sermon is the goal of preachers who have not abandoned their own listening.

Listen.
    Listen to the sounds in the sanctuary.
Throats clearing. Weight shifting. Children's loud whispers.
    Listen to the sounds of
        Anticipation.

The organ key accidentally pushed as the organist leaves her post.
Listen to the minds.
    Bills to pay.
        Friend to counsel.
            Dinner to plan.
Doubts. Needs. Hopes. Dreams. Worries. Fears.
And the preacher. Listen. Quiet now. Waiting.

The gift is coming.

    The gift of the spoken word.

What meanings will be made?

Connection? Contentment? Inspiration? Insight? Transformation?

The silent moment before the sermon. Expectation. Listen.

Listen to the words.

Words in one mind.

    Spoken words.

        Words times infinity in the minds of others.

Listen.                        Listen to the words.

# Notes

[1] Advertisment. (January/February, 1999). *Preaching*, 18.

[2] Dance, F.E.X., & Zak-Dance, C. (1994). *Speaking your mind: Private thinking and public speech*. Dubuque, IA: Kendall-Hunt Publishing Company, 45–46.

[3] See Sprague, J. & Stuart, D. (1996). *The speaker's handbook* (4th ed.). Fort Worth, TX: Harcourt Brace College Publishers, 41–42.

[4] Farris, S. (1998). *Preaching that matters: The Bible and our lives*. Louisville, KY: Westminster John Knox Press.

[5] Tisdale, L.T. (1997). *Preaching as local theology and folk art*. Minneapolis, MN: Fortress Press, xi.

[6] See Sprague, & Stuart, 42.

[7] See Tisdale.

[8] See Farris, 8.

[9] See Dance, & Zak-Dance, 127

[10] See Dance, & Zak-Dance, 115.

[11] See Dance, & Zak Dance, 115.

[12] See Dance, & Zak-Dance, 22.

[13] Lucado, M. (1997). *The great house of God*. Dallas, TX: Word Publishing, 83.

[14] Menzel, K.E., & Carrell, L.J. (1994). "The relationship between preparation and performance in public speaking." *Communication Education*, 43, 17–26.

# SECTION 4

# TRANSFORMATION

*"It is important that action be taken in living the faith. Beliefs are not enough."*

A LISTENER

Chapter 10

# The Gift Is Ours

We know that words cannot move mountains, but
they can move the multitude . . . Words shape
thought, stir feelings, and beget action, they kill
and revive, corrupt and cure. The 'men of
words'—priests, prophets, intellectuals—have
played a more decisive role in history than mili-
tary leaders, statesmen, and businessmen.
—Eric Hoffer[1]

LET'S REVIEW the theoretical premises of this book.
- Spoken words are uniquely human, symbolic, and
  *potentially powerful.*
- Communication is a *mutual* endeavor to co-create
  meaning.
- The primary function of human communication is that *we
  affect one another.* The spoken word has an inherent transformative function.

And what do we know about the realities of the communicative
act of preaching in the United States?
- Millions listen weekly.
- Hundreds of thousands preach.
- Listeners and preachers generally do not approach the ser-
  mon as communication partners, though such is the case.
- There are varying degrees of communication competence
  among these sermon partners.

231

- There is little dialogue among listeners and preachers about sermons.

And, as we will learn in this chapter,

- Preachers believe their sermons are counter-cultural.

**The communicative act called "sermon" is indeed potentially transformative.** But who is being transformed? And how? To what end? What is it in the culture that is being countered? Is the message of Jesus Christ transformative? The preachers and listeners say, "Yes." Is the spoken word a potentially powerful change agent? The communication professor says, "Yes." Given that potential transformative power of both the message and the human process of spoken interaction, will the meanings being created in sermon communication at the turn of the millennium actually play a "decisive role in history" (as Hoffer suggests in the quotation which opens this chapter)? Our examination of sermon communication through the lens of a communication perspective leads us to conclude that **the preaching act itself needs to be transformed if the potential power of the sermon is to be maximized.** We have grossly underestimated the potential power of the sermon in those millions of listeners' lives. Why do we let this continue?

Most listeners do not participate in sermon communication anticipating that they will be changed. Preachers and listeners can be paralyzed by low expectancy, trapped in a self-perpetuating cycle. For millions, comfort creates an increasingly self-centered faith. Some preachers defend ineffectual preaching with religious precepts or "blame the listener" mentalities. Some listeners accept the lack of transformation as normal.

In *Why Christian: For Those on the Edge of Faith*, J.D. Hall says, "It is my impression . . . that the greatest misunderstandings of Christianity present in our American and Canadian context today are misunderstandings perpetrated and perpetuated by Christian bodies themselves."[2] Is it possible that sermons themselves perpetuate these "misunderstandings"?:

- Sermons are irrelevant? (So Christianity is irrelevant.)
- Sermons are impractical? (So Christianity is impractical.)

- Sermons promote passive listeners? (So Christianity is passive.)
- We don't expect much from sermon communication? (So we don't expect much from Christianity.)

Interviewed preachers were asked, "How would things be different if everyone who'd ever heard you preach believed the message and put the words into action?" The responses included:

- "Everyone would be a lot nicer."
- "Life would slow down."
- "Everyone would live by the Golden Rule."
- "Fewer people would be grumpy."
- "Other drivers wouldn't give you the finger."
- "You wouldn't have to lock your doors."
- "People would be friendlier."
- "It would be a really nice world."

Are these the goals for which the power of the spoken word is being squandered during the billions of minutes devoted to sermon communication? Sure, a nicer world would be, well, "nice," but is that the message of the Christian gospel? Is that the objective of preaching in the Christian church at the turn of the millennium? Niceness?

On the other end of the continuum, two of the interviewed preachers responded to the "How would things be different?" question with visions of radical, revolutionary, cultural change they called "revival." Said one, a Protestant pastor from a mainline denomination: "We would experience another great revival. It would be more incredible than any revival in history. The difference would be so great that we cannot even picture it." And the other, a Catholic priest, proclaimed: "It would be too much to even imagine. It would be so completely different from what we experience now. We wouldn't even recognize our society. Remember that *Star Trek* episode when a frozen guy was found floating in a spaceship? When they unfroze him, he wanted to be in touch with his bank. Captain Picard told him 'We learned centuries ago how to manage without banks. We've outgrown our need for money.' The frozen guy experienced some culture shock. That's what it would be like for us. A whole new world. Unrecognizable."

Among the preachers in the survey who identified "change" as their consistent sermon goal, there is great variance in the types of changes they are attempting to instigate. Following is a list that summarizes the preachers' responses to the question about the potential transformative effect of sermons. As we examine this list, let's remember to be asking three crucial questions:

(1) Which messages are actually counter-cultural?
(2) What is the relationship of the church, the individual listeners, and the broader culture?
(3) For such radical transformation to occur, how must the sermon itself be transformed?

Keeping these questions in mind, let's consider the interviewed preachers' perspectives regarding the potential kinds of transformations their sermons could create.

### Individuals would:

- "Make a decision to believe the gospel message."
- "Make their spirituality an extremely high life priority."
- "Extend forgiveness to self and others."
- "Be more Christ-like."
- "Buy less, give more, becoming non-materialistic."
- "Share the story of Jesus."
- "Grow in self-esteem."
- "Move away from narcissism, becoming more conscious of the needs of others."
- "See the value of other people's reality; more acceptance of all other people as people God loves."
- "Read the Scripture regularly for guidance."
- "Pray seriously, and not just for themselves."
- "Read Christian authors."
- "Experience lots more joy."
- "Lessen fear and feelings of defeatism."
- "Take responsibility for their own actions; stop blaming others."

- "Feel free, not trapped."
- "Live lives permeated with sacrificial love."

## Families would:
- "Become more forgiving."
- "Be more healthy; less dysfunctional."
- "Demonstrate more love."
- "Teach young people to look after the elderly."
- "Encourage the elderly to share stories with young people."
- "Experience greater harmony."
- "Seek better communication."
- "Produce children who are respectful of parents and elders."
- "Affirm one another."
- "Respect one another."

## Churches would:
- "Experience reconciliation."
- "Become a community."
- "Behave like a healthy family."
- "Be a group of people passionate about discovering God's will for our lives."
- "Be a group of people passionate about sharing the Good News of Christ with our friends."
- "Have greater participation in service opportunities."
- "Break down walls of denominationalism."
- "Take back our responsibility for orphans and widows (not dump them on the state)."

## The broader cultural system would:
- "Experience reconciliation."
- "Have the Senate doing something else today" (written in January 1999, during the Clinton impeachment trial).
- "Become a loving, caring place."
- "Change its economic system to lessen the degree of difference between the 'haves' and 'have nots.'"
- "Become more socially, racially, and economically inclusive."

- "Change its moral state."
- "End hunger."
- "End homelessness."
- "Stop the prejudice, hate, and even violence that have been justified in the name of Christianity in this country."
- "Lower its crime rate."
- "Become a nation of servants."
- "Experience another great revival."

Obviously, preachers believe transformation is possible. For example, interviewed preachers' most commonly mentioned goal was *reconciliation*—at all levels—individual, family, church, and broader culture. Experiencing grace themselves and stimulated by their sermons, could listeners "revive" their families and communities through active processes of reconciliation? Why not? Preachers and listeners must create high expectations for the transformation they seek.

The spoken word is powerful enough to enable such transformation. Reconciliation is needed, and the message of Jesus is consistent with the message of reconciliation. In his book, *Forgive: Healing the Hurts We Don't Deserve*, Lewis Smedes concludes, "When we forgive we ride the crest of love's cosmic wave; we walk in stride with God."[3]

Before your author naively promotes such an agenda, she must listen to the voices of preachers whose conflict about the appropriate nature of change for Christians has itself been a divisive force. Perhaps reconciliation between the "change the person" and "change the society" perspectives is needed before increases in transformation become a reality. Says one interviewed preacher when answering the transformation question, "The change could be a personal, subtle thing. If you change the person, you change the home, the community—the nation—the world. Such change would not be rooted in my preaching ability but in the power of the gospel message." Of course the inward and outward changes are linked. Why one to the exclusion of the other?

Says James H. Evans, Jr. in his 1997 book, *We Shall All Be Changed*, "The irony of our times [is that] we fail to connect our desire for spiritual renewal to our need for social transformation."[4] He also asserts, "Authentic liberation from the forces of sin and death requires both personal spiritual transformation and public social transformation."[5] To some in the church, the divide between those preachers (and sermons) that seek personal spiritual transformation and those which seek public social transformation is a divide as striking as the Grand Canyon is to the bridge builder. In his work, *Preaching Jesus*, homiletics professor Charles Campbell claims,

> Most of the sermons I hear focus either on the needs of individuals in the congregation or on issues in American society . . . reflecting a story that divides life into the "private" and the "public" with no room for the church (and with Christianity increasingly relegated to the private realm because of its lack of influence on the public).[6]

Campbell goes on to argue that the purpose of the sermon should be interpreted communally, within the context of the church community. He asserts that a focus on building a community of faith within the church is "radically different" than either the "individual felt needs" or the "societal change" approaches.

Such is the premise of the work of Hauerwas and Willimon in *Resident Aliens* as well. They separate churches into three types:
(1) The *activist* church, working to build a better society, a "new kingdom" on earth.
(2) The *conversionist* church, working for inward changes in individual believers.
(3) The *confessing* church, a "radical alternative."

Hauerwas and Willimon explain that while the activist church accepts the culture and the conversionist church rejects the culture, the "confessing" option is a "counter cultural social structure called church" which knows that "its most credible form of witness (and the most 'effective' thing it can do for the world) is the actual creation of a living breathing, visible community of faith." [7]

This suggestion that the broader culture be countered with a model of a culture (the church) which represents the ideal of the Christian kingdom is a powerful idea. Can the church become such an entity? Sacrificial love, reconciliation, mercy, justice, communal care—do such practices characterize the church? Or do we model the broader culture's individualistic self-centeredness, materialism, conflict, injustice, and ethnocentrism?

Imagine a conservative preacher in a small town who explains Scripture passages for 45 minutes each Sunday, a Catholic priest at a politically liberal campus parish who performs song and story using inductive logic in his short homilies, an evangelical pastor of a large seeker-sensitive church who quotes regularly from *The Wall Street Journal*, an inner city preacher whose focus is the fight against racial injustice, and lots of other preachers from various traditions gathered in one room to talk about preaching. Can you predict one idea to which they would all agree? This sermon survey research found at least one: **Preaching is counter-cultural.**

In her work *Comforting One Another in Life's Sorrows*, Karen Mains envisions such a "confessional" church using the metaphor of the pietá, which she defines as "any person or group of persons holding a body in death or a body near death. In its broadest sense a pietá is any time we give comfort to those trampled by life's sorrows."[8] She begins with the now familiar photo of firefighter Chris Fields holding the body of one-year-old Baylee Almon pulled from the wreckage of the Oklahoma City bombing. After describing pietás in literature and art, deriving principles for "holding one another," Mains asserts, "I feel strongly that the role of Christ's people is to provide a protective circle around those who are suffering, whether from their own ill-doing or from circumstances beyond their control . . . The greatest of transgressions is for Christ's people to abandon those in trouble."[9] A vision of a church experiencing mercy and extending mercy to all those it touches is a vision of a church not derailed by a "personal" versus "social" dichotomy. Such a church would indeed be "counter-cultural" in the term's most positive sense. Yes, there is the vision of a church whose sermons and resulting actions are truly transformative. As one preacher said, "In a culture transformed by the Christian gospel, no one would ever die alone from AIDS."

Some will say that delineating churches into types is artificial. Perhaps some churches are already "doing it all"—inviting personal transformation to result in a church community that replicates God's intent for human interaction, allowing a model for the broader culture that inspires its transformation as well. Others see a Protestant church divided along racial lines, with the black church more socially-minded than the white church—a racially divided church needing to learn from one another, a racially divided church needing reconciliation. Says G. Wilmore, author of *Black and Presbyterian*,

> How can the black church use the history, culture and experience of their historic struggle for freedom, to enhance the proclamation of the gospel of Jesus Christ and the manifestation of his power to transform not only black humanity, but the whole human race?[10]

It seems conversionist churches may decry the "hypocrisy" of an activist church that ignores application of Christianity to the personal lifestyle. Imagine a person who interprets all sermonic meanings in relation to the broader culture, working tirelessly for social justice yet treating family and colleagues with disdain, committing adultery, breaking confidences, and demeaning those who disagree. On the other hand, those in activist churches may complain that a self-focused Christian who spends life striving for inward holiness may end up ignoring the realities of the human condition. A Christian who reads the Bible daily yet demonstrates ignorance regarding the racism, poverty, and violence in our culture seems to the activist a hypocrite as well. Add to these divisions the terms "liberal" and "conservative" and the separation widens even further.

"Will Christian action be directed inward or outward?" seems a limiting question. Rather, let's ask the transformative question, "Why not both?" The "either/or" mentality separates Christians rather than furthering the reconciling power of the Christian message. Parker Palmer's work explores the tensions between private and public manifestations of Christian experience. He concludes,

"If we are to renew our outward action by deepening our inward quest, we must first learn to see the inner and outer as two halves of the whole."[11] Indeed, when Barna describes revival, he cites Charles Finney and Tom Phillips who say that we know revival has come when "cultural change is evident and is attributable to widespread individual spiritual transformation."[12]

Say Hauerwas and Willimon, "The challenge facing Christians is . . . to form a community, a colony of resident aliens, which is so shaped by our convictions that no one ever has to ask what we mean by confessing belief in God as Father, Son, and Holy Spirit. The biggest problem facing Christian theology is not translation, but enactment."[13] Let us not forget that the premise for this book is that the potential of the spoken sermon is utterly transformative.

"Show me how this connects to my life," says the listener. We are not the first to struggle with the church-culture relationship. How does Christian meaning connect to daily living? Certainly the early church was counter-cultural, a small group supporting one another as they were persecuted by the powerful. With Constantine's conversion, Christianity became socially sanctioned and violence was then justified in the name of Truth. In the early middle ages, the church and many of its members withdrew from culture into monasteries to practice their faith privately. This struggle of Christians to reconcile their relationship with the broader culture has gone on through the ages and is not likely to end soon.

Though the theological bases for various church traditions have been represented quite simply here, this "divide" has been mentioned because those who preach and those who listen need to have clarity about their goals for transformation. Are we just trying to be nicer? Okay, let's be nicer. Are we into a cycle of continual affirmation and approval, not perceiving a need for transformation? Okay, then we can minimize the power of the spoken word and the power of the gospel message with mediocrity and complacency. But wouldn't we rather set higher goals? Preachers. Listeners. Is transformation your goal?

In his book, *Blinded by the Might: The Rise and Fall of the Moral Majority*, Cal Thomas admits:

> Two decades after conservative Christians charged into the political arena, bringing new voters and millions of dollars with them in hopes of transforming the culture through political power, it must now be acknowledged that we have failed. We failed not because we were wrong about our critique of culture, or because we lacked conviction, or because there were not enough of us, or because too many were lethargic and uncommitted. We failed because we were unable to redirect a nation from the top down. Real change must come from the bottom up or, better yet, from the inside out.[14]

When conservative Christian Paul Weyrich recently declared that moral conservatives should "separate ourselves from this hostile culture" and that "politics have failed," Washington Post writer E.J. Dione responded with this perception, "If Weyrich's new strategy makes religious conservatives less an interest group and more a leaven in our national life, he may discover that the culture is less hostile to their values than he thinks."[15]

What are the values of dominant U.S. culture? What do the sermons of the Christian church try to counter? "The single most important pattern in the United States is individualism," say authors of the textbook, *Communication Between Cultures*.[16] Individualism manifests itself in *individual initiative* ("Pull yourself up by your own boot straps"), *independence* ("Do your own thing"), *individual expression* ("The squeaky wheel gets the grease"), and *privacy* ("A man's home is his castle").[17]

"A society could not last a single day if its people were motivated by nothing except the maximization of self-interest,"[18] says Robert Bellah. And yet, we citizens of the United States seem to be attempting to do just that, with some notable exceptions. Can we claim that most sermons counter this cultural pattern of individualism? Says J. Wallis in his *Agenda for a Biblical People*,

> An individualistic understanding of the gospel carries the danger of making salvation into just

another commodity that can be consumed for
personal fulfillment and self-interest, for a guarantee of happiness, success, moral justification,
or whatever else a consumer audience feels it
needs.[19]

In a conflict class I was teaching, a discussion of domestic abuse
led to some fairly frank revelations by several of the students. In
the mood to self-disclose, one young man said, "I've never known
anyone who has been abused or who has abused someone else."
The statement was met with a chorus of groans from many in the
class. Feeling defensive, the young man continued, "Why is domestic abuse something I need to study? It doesn't affect me."
Attempting to guide his thinking, I responded, "If your neighbor
abuses his wife and children, does domestic abuse affect you?" I'm
sure the color drained from my face as he became entrenched in
his position. "No," he said. "That's his business." A few angry
class members began to pummel him with verbal challenges: "One
of those abused children may grow up to murder or molest your
children." "Your own children will learn your lack of concern for
others if you ignore what's happening next door." No matter what
was said, the young man, now a college graduate, could not conceive of his connectedness to others or his need to move beyond
individualistic concerns. Such self-centeredness directly contradicts
the other-centeredness that is integral to the Christian faith.

Our ultimate commands as Christians—to love God and others—are commands that require a greater degree of collectivism
than U.S. culture supports. Those commands reconcile the per-
sonal-social "dilemma" as well! Because we love God and experience God's love, we extend that love to others. This love is not
merely "niceness" but sacrificial, other-centered behavior that includes a kind of forgiveness and mercy-giving not common in the
broader culture of our day. Says R.A. Swenson, author of *The
Overload Syndrome,*

We were put here for love. There isn't any theological dispute about it—love is the goal of the
Christian life. Scripture teaches us that God is

love. It teaches us that the greatest commandment
is to love. It teaches us that all the command-
ments are summed up in the one commandment
to love. It teaches us that without love, we are
nothing.[20]

Sacrificial love demands an other-focus rather than a self-focus.
Do our sermons teach us how we can counter the cultural forces
that carry us out into the sea of individualism? Says J.D. Hall, in
his "conversation" with a non-believing friend, "You omit that love
profoundly challenges our self-centeredness . . . The commitment
that goes with *real* love is *real* commitment."[21]

Materialism is another of the dominant U.S. cultural patterns.
Those preachers who champion other ways of living, such as Tony
Campolo, are considered radicals in many Christian circles; perhaps respected, but not often modeled. Certainly, Christianity is
counter to materialism. Do our sermons counter materialism's effects? Or do we accept that such a cultural wave is so strong, the
church could not possibly paddle a life raft full of Christians against
that current? One interviewed preacher said, "My last sermon was
on consumerism. I don't have the slightest delusion that anything
I say is going to make a difference, but I'm going to say it anyway."

Why not? Why can't such a sermon make a difference? U.S.
culture also values progress, technology, competition, youth, and
activity. In what ways does the Christian message interact with
such patterns? Do they need to be countered, confirmed, or just
thoroughly considered? Do sermons result in co-created meanings
which counter other-interest over self-interest? Being vs. doing?
Spiritual vs. material? Justice vs. injustice? Sacrificial love vs. indifference? Forgiveness vs. resentment and retaliation? Or do listeners make their meanings about such topics from their experiences
totally outside the Christian context? "Well, if she's an alcoholic,
he should just leave her. He's *enabling* her behavior by missing
work to take care of the kids while she sleeps it off." In this man's
life challenge, perhaps he needs a mercy-giver from his church to
assist him in the practical love of his children so he does not lose
the job that supports them. Is the church organized around the

culture's individualistic patterns ("It's his problem to solve") or around life-changing precepts of faith that challenge self-determined models? What have the listeners gained through the sermons that will allow them to respond to the lives of others in Christlike fashion?

Oh yes, it gets complicated to open ourselves to transformation. It gets scary. Even overwhelming. Says a listener, "My heart just bleeds for the Kosovo refugees but I can't quit my job to go help; I have responsibilities to my children. Every social crisis calls out to me. As a Christian, I know I should respond, but I don't have time, money, or a way to be involved. I just end up throwing five bucks here and five bucks there to help prisoners, refugees, or the homeless."

The church can struggle to provide means for more personal and practical involvement in individual, family, community, and social crises. Surely having every Christian move to Calcutta to serve those poor and needy would leave great gaps. Said a talented preschool teacher, "I just really want to do something important with my life. I want to be a world-changer." Since my daughter had directly benefited from this teacher's active, consistent love, I wanted to shout back to her (though I restrained myself), "You *are* a world changer! We need you to keep doing what you are doing. This *is* important."

We cannot all do everything. For some, life circumstances are so difficult and resources are so limited that survival or faithfulness become the primary goals. For others, gifts and opportunities open doors to specific types of service with broader impact. Says J.D. Hall to his unbelieving friend, "You asked what difference is made by the Christian faith, and finally, I think . . . It depends on who you are, what you are called to be and become . . . Your life, if you become a Christian, will be the answer."[22] Will an individual's manifestations of Christianity be more church-directed, more society-directed, or more inner-directed? The answers will be based in the merger of each person with the spiritual messages that he encounters, including those created during sermon communication.

According to the listeners, preachers often talk to them as if they are opponents rather than supporters. In his book,

*Christopraxis: A Theology of Action*, Edmund Arens provides a helpful examination of the approaches Jesus took as he spoke to various constituencies:

(1)  With the concretely needy and marginalized, Jesus provides concrete assistance and works to relieve their suffering.

(2)  With competitors and opponents like the Pharisees, Jesus seeks dialogue, and "measures the Pharisees' teachings by what they actually do."

(3)  With supporters and adherents, Jesus surrounds himself with them so that they become part of his communicative action. (Arens notes the diversity of Jesus' supporters.)

(4)  With people in general (the population in the area of his activity—the community), Jesus connects with the powerless; they are the characters in his parables and the models for the beatitudes.[23]

The communication of Jesus had an other-orientation. He did not approach any group in the culture with disdain, nor did he separate himself from those who sought him out. Though the culture to which U.S. sermons must connect at the turn of the millennium is dramatically different than that of the time and place of Jesus, the need for connection that comes from an "other-orientation" has not changed. The need for the preacher to decenter the sermon through the perspective of the listener has not changed. And this other-centeredness in the sermon is part of the transformation that sermon communication needs. While thus far this chapter has attempted to lead the reader in thinking through the idea of "transformation" as the goal of the sermon, the book as a whole is about the transformation of sermon communication itself.

Based on the responses of listeners and preachers across the United States, it is argued here that for the transformative power of the spoken words of a sermon to have maximum impact, many preachers and listeners need to change their communicative behaviors. Most of those who participated in the study are not satisfied with the current state of preaching. This book is full of suggestions from preachers to listeners, replete with advice from listeners to preachers, and teeming with recommendations from speech communication research.

But for actual sermon transformation to occur, preacher, listener, you must see the need, set a goal, and begin the hard work of mastering the steps that lead toward that change. If you believe in the power of the message and believe in the power of the spoken word, then the motivation to change your own sermon communication behavior seems a logical outcome of this process of reflecting about preaching. Could the words of a sermon actually spur listeners to seek reconciliation in all aspects of their lives? Where would the effect of such meanings end? The possibilities are almost beyond imagination. Says the preacher expecting revival, expecting transformation, "Such has been the kingdom vision of Christian reformers since the time of Christ. In every generation God raises up those who strongly believe that something like this can happen." How do preachers and listeners cocreate meanings that transform? How does one become a more competent communicator?

I challenge you to go back through each chapter of this book, looking for *specific* communicative goals to set. Rudolph Verderber suggests a goal statement which

- describes the problem
- identifies a specific, measurable goal in one sentence
- lists procedural steps necessary to reach the goal
- identifies how to determine if the goal has been attained.

He also suggests that you sign and date the document, with a witness present![24] I like to call such a witness the "accountability" partner.

In general, listeners and preachers need to find a way to create and sustain dialogue about their sermon communication. Listeners and preachers need to accept their mutual responsibility in the co-creation of meaning. Listeners and preachers must abandon the monologue mindset that sustains the cycle of listener passivity, preacher disconnection, and sermon irrelevancy. And, listeners and preachers must believe in the power of the spoken word to be transformative.

A listener survey has arrived in the mail today, four months past the deadline, but right on time for these ending moments. The listener provides this "one message" to all the preachers in the United States:

> Bring the Truth of Jesus in love to the people. Love the people in the church. Know the people in the community. Develop ways to connect the local people with the world by being aware of the greater scope of things. Empower the congregation to be difference-makers, not just pew-sitters. Step up the challenges. Offer steps to reach those goals.

How can such goals be accomplished? A gift has been given. A gift that can produce positive, powerful transformation. The uniquely human capacity—the gift of the spoken word. Yes, indeed, words can change moments, words can change lives. Words can wound, and words can incite reconciliation. The spoken word has impact. Preachers, listeners, the gift is yours. How will you use the gift of the spoken word to affect one another?

## Notes

[1] Quotation from social philosopher Eric Hoffer, documented at the following web site: http://www.bomis.com/cgi-binl/ ring.cgi?page=2&ring=twainquotes.

[2] Hall, J.D. (1998). *Why Christian: For those on the edge of faith.* Minneapolis, MN: Augsburg Fortress Press, 175.

[3] Smedes, L.B. (1984). *Forgive: Healing the hurts we don't deserve.* New York: Pocket Books, 192.

[4] Evans, J.H. (1997). *We shall all be changed.* Minneapolis, MN: Augsburg Fortress Press, 104.

[5] See Evans, 104.

[6] Campbell, C.L. (1997). *Preaching Jesus: New directions for homiletics in Hans Frei's postliberal theology.* Grand Rapids, MI: William B. Eerdmans Publishing Company, 230–231.

[7] Hauerwas, S., & Willimon, W.H. (1989). *Resident Aliens.* Nashville, TN: Abingdon Press, 44–47.

[8] Mains, K. (1997). *Comforting one another in life's sorrows.* Nashville, TN: Thomas Nelson Publishers.

[9] See Mains, 154–155.

[10] Wilmore, G. (1983). *Black and Presbyterian: The heritage and the hope.* Philadelphia, PA: Geneva Press, 84.

[11] Palmer, P. (1981). *The company of strangers: Christians and the renewal of America's public life.* New York: Crossroad, 156.

[12] Barna, G. (1999, January). Report to Promise Keepers Organization, Colorado Springs, CO. Same study was also documented in October 27, 1998 news release with contact person David Kinnaman listed, phone number (805) 658-8885.

[13] See Hauerwas, & Willimon, 170–171.

[14] Thomas, C. (March 28, 1999). Excerpt from the book *Blinded by the might: The rise and fall of the moral majority.* Reprinted in the *Oshkosh Northwestern,* Oshkosh, WI.

[15] Dione, E.J. (March 14, 1999). *Historic grounding for separatist remarks.* Reprinted in the *Oshkosh Northwestern,* Oshkosh, WI.

[16] Samovar, L.A., Porter, R.E., & Stefani, L.A. (1998). *Communication between cultures* (3rd ed.). Belmont, CA: Wadsworth Pub-

lishing Company, 62.

[17] See Samovar, Porter, & Stefani, 62.

[18] Bellah, R. (1978, Fall). "Commentary and proposed agenda: The normative framework for pluralism in America." *Soundings, LXI*, 3.

[19] Wallis, J. (1976). *Agenda for a Biblical people.* New York: Harper and Row.

[20] Swenson, R.A. (1998). *The overload syndrome: Learning to live within your limits.* Colorado Springs, CO: Navpress, 195.

[21] See Hall, 112.

[22] See Hall, 103.

[23] Arens, E. (1995). *Christopraxis: A theology of action.* Translated by J.F. Hoffmeyer. Minneapolis, MN: Fortress Press.

[24] Verderber, R. (1996). *Communicate!* (8th ed.). Belmont, CA: Wadsworth Publishing, 23–24.

# Index